Optimi
European Union
Law

OPTIMIZE LAW REVISION

The Optimize series' academic advisors are:

– Michael Bromby, Higher Education Academy Discipline Lead for Law 2011–2013, Reader in Law, GCU.
'The use of visualisation in Optimize will help students to focus on the key issues when revising.'

– Emily Allbon, Law Librarian and creator of Lawbore, City University.

'Partnering well-explained, comprehensive content with visual tools like maps and flowcharts is what makes the Optimize series so unique. These books help students take their learning up a notch; offering support in grappling with the subject, as well as insight into what will help make their work stand out.'

– Sanmeet Kaur Dua, Lecturer in Law, co-creator of Lawbore, City University.

'This series sets out the essential concepts and principles that students need to grasp in a logical way by combining memorable visual diagrams and text. Students will find that they will not easily forget what they read in this series as the unique aim higher and interaction points will leave a blueprint in their minds.'

– Zoe Swan, Senior Lecturer in Law, University of Brighton.

'The wide range of visual material includes diagrams, charts, tables and maps enable students to check their knowledge and understanding on each topic area, every step of the way... When combined with carefully explained legal principles and solid, understandable examples, students will find this series provides them with a win- win solution to the study of law and developing revision techniques.'

Optimize European Union Law

Glenn Robinson

Routledge
Taylor & Francis Group

LONDON AND NEW YORK

First published 2014
by Routledge
2 Park Square, Milton Park, Abingdon, Oxon OX14 4RN

and by Routledge
711 Third Avenue, New York, NY 10017

Routledge is an imprint of the Taylor & Francis Group, an informa business
© 2014 Glenn Robinson

British Library Cataloguing in Publication Data
A catalogue record for this book is available from the British Library

Library of Congress Cataloging in Publication Data
A catalog record for this book has been requested

ISBN: 978-0-415-83464-3 (pbk)
ISBN: 978-1-315-84901-0 (ebk)

Typeset in TheSans
by RefineCatch Limited, Bungay, Suffolk

Printed and bound by CPI Group (UK) Ltd, Croydon, CR0 4YY

Contents

Optimize – Your Blueprint for Exam Success

Why Optimize?

In developing the *Optimize* format, Routledge have spent a lot of time talking to law lecturers and examiners about assessment, teaching and learning and exam preparation. The aim of our series is to help you make the most of your knowledge to gain good marks – to optimize your revision.

Students

Students told us that there was a huge amount to learn and that visual features such as diagrams, tables and flowcharts made the law easier to follow. Learning and remembering cases was an area of difficulty, as was applying these in problem questions. Revision guides could make this easier by presenting to law succinctly, showing concepts in a visual format and highlighting how important cases can be applied in assessment.

Lecturers

Lecturers agreed that visual features were effective to aid learning, but were concerned that students learned by rote when using revision guides. To succeed in assessment, they wanted to encourage them to get their teeth into arguments, to support their answers with authority and show they had truly understood the principles underlying their questions. In short, they wanted them to show they understood how they were assessed on the law, rather than repeating the basic principles.

Assessment criteria

If you want to do well in exams, it's important to understand how you will be assessed. In order to get the best out of your exam or essay question, your first port of call should be to make yourself familiar with the marking criteria available from your law school; this will help you to identify and recognise the skills and knowledge you will need to succeed. Like course outlines, assessment criteria can differ from school to school and so if you can get hold of a copy of your own criteria, this will be invaluable. To give you a clear idea of what these criteria look like, we've collated the most common terms from 64 marking schemes for core curriculum courses in the UK.

reading

Evidence

Understanding

Structure   Critical Argument

sources

Application

Knowledge

Presentation

Common Assessment Criteria, Routledge Subject Assessment Survey

Optimizing the law

The format of this Optimize Law volume has been developed with these assessment criteria and the learning needs of students firmly in mind.

❖ **Visual format**: Our expert series advisors have brought a wealth of knowledge about visual learning to help us to develop the books' visual format.

❖ **Tailored coverage**: Each book is tailored to the needs of your core curriculum course and presents all commonly taught topics.

❖ **Assessment led-revision**: Our authors are experienced teachers with an interest in how students learn, and they have structured each chapter around revision objectives that relate to the criteria you will be assessed on.

❖ **Assessment led-pedagogy**: The Aim Higher, Common Pitfalls, Up for Debate and Case precedent features used in these books are closely linked to common assessment criteria – showing you how to gain the best marks, avoid the worst, apply the law and think critically about it.

❖ **Putting it into practice**: Each chapter presents example essay or problem questions and template answers to show you how to apply what you have learned.

Routledge and the Optimize team wish you the very best of luck in your exams and essays!

Preface

For many students EU law can be a challenge; at times, the perceived legislative density of this essentially civil law subject can appear impenetrable. One of the aims of this text is to provide a way in to this subject by providing the key information in a series of manageable steps allowing the reader to walk through the most essential topics in a visual and stimulating way.

As most students will be familiar with the common law approach with the focus on case law precedent and the relative rigidity of the *stare decisis* doctrine, it is worth explaining at this point how EU law departs from the binding precedent template and to emphasise the importance of legislation in this system.

In one important way, EU law differs from UK law in that the use of precedent in the overwhelming majority of Member States within the union is persuasive; the judiciary are guided by previous cases, but are not necessarily bound to follow them. In this European approach, the case can be followed by the judge, but there is a greater freedom about the choices and pathways available in the judicial decision-making process.

Another notable difference between the two systems, the UK common law and the civil law prevalent in mainland Europe is the role of statutes or as they are more commonly termed within the EU Member States, codes. Whereas, in the UK, a statute is typically written in a detailed way with precise definitions where possible, in Europe and as we shall see in the EU, the legislation acts a starting point for the judiciary to interpret and apply in an arguably more dynamic way.

As I am sure you know, in the UK, the traditional approach to statutory interpretation has always been the literal rule, the so-called 'dictionary rule' which compels the judge to produce meanings for the words in the statute which are arguably limited to the obvious, literal meanings of the words. This can lead to absurdities where the clear literal meaning is out of date or does not produce the intended outcome which the statute was designed to achieve. Jurisprudence is littered with many such examples.

By way of contrast, the European approach has developed along teleological lines and has come to be known commonly in the UK as the 'purposive' rule. Using this tool, the European judge will focus on the reason for the legislation. Broadly speaking, instead of asking the question: What does the statute say? A European judge will ask: What is the purpose of the code?

This approach throws up some interesting issues relating to the role of the judge in Europe and the way in which legislation is produced in the EU Member States and, by extension, the EU itself.

Starting with the first issue: the role of the judge. In the Court of Justice of the European Union, the judges will treat the legislation in front of them as a 'living document' to be interpreted and upgraded as social circumstances and legal necessity demand. For example, in 1957 in the original Treaty of Rome, sex discrimination was provided for in only a limited way. The original Article 119 (now Article 157 TFEU), merely stated that men and women should have equal pay.

This legal area developed greatly over the years through a progressive series of judgments which drove the law forward and expanded the notion of sex discrimination. Over this period, issues such as work of equal value, discrimination against pregnant women, equal rights for those who have changed gender or have been discriminated against on the grounds of their sexuality have all been raised and formed the basis for judgments in the European Court. Through this purposive approach, the original EU law has been re-interpreted in line with prevailing contemporary attitudes without the need to change the legislation at all.

However, this leads on to my next point, concerning the role of legislation. First, the law in the EU does clearly change over time. The cases outlined above in relation to sex discrimination have led to revisions in the EU through new Treaty articles, or the introduction of regulations or directives. This usually happens following a sequence of cases which have flagged up an area as especially complex or in need of clarification. Here, the legislation fulfils the roles of law reform and codification of the case law.

Second, in regard to legislation, it is worth noting that, in contrast to UK statutes, EU law is worded in a 'looser', less precise and less definitive manner. This allows the judiciary greater freedom in their approach and is typical of the European, civil law modus operandi. In this way, through a combination of the mode of language deployed, the persuasive use of precedent and the purposive interpretative approach, the law of the EU continues to develop and grow to meet the challenges of an ever-growing Union.

There is a further introductory point to make.

The law-making powers of the institution and the interpretative powers of the judiciary are bounded. This is in line with the approach prevalent in a common law system.

In the UK, common law is driven forward by the courts, hence the name, 'judge-made' law. It is possible for law to be taken in unexpected directions and, when there is no obvious precedent or it is clearly time for a change, it is now accepted that British judges enjoy some freedom in this area.

Arguably, this is not the case in the EU. The Treaties as outlined in the next chapter act as the starting point for the law to develop. This operates in two ways.

First, when new secondary legislation is planned, it must emerge from the foundation treaty: put simply, the EU could not produce legislation on free movement of goods unless a Treaty article on this area was already in existence.

Second, when deciding cases, the judges of the CJEU must produce judgments which sit within the overarching EU legal framework of Treaty Articles, and secondary legislation.

This means that the common law freedom arguably enjoyed by judges in the UK is not available to their colleagues in the EU. The closest topics to the common law approach are arguably those of direct effect, indirect effect and state liability where the judges creatively introduced these doctrines. However, in all three, justification for the judicial approach was found within the body of the treaties – again illustrating the bounded nature of the EU system.

In terms of learning the law contained in this text, there is a very useful approach which my students have found helpful in 'seeing' their way through.

When asked a legal question relating to UK law, the habitual answer of the student is to cite case law and precedent. This needs to be modified when studying EU law.

When you are asked a similar question on EU law – you should invariably start with the Treaty Article relating to that area. As you will note in the majority of the following chapters, each topic area cites the relevant Treaty Articles first. This is important as the primary legislation, the Article, will lay out the framework for the area and provide the requisite legal permission for secondary legislation to be introduced to broaden out the area and fill in any gaps which appear as the law is used and applied.

Once the relevant Article has been engaged, two routes of exploration open up. First, what are the key cases relating to that Article – how has the legal content of the Article been interpreted and applied in the courts? Each Article thus has associated case law whereby the judges tell us what the language of the Article means. As noted previously, these judgments are persuasive and can change over time.

Second, once you have an overview of the base Articles and their interpreting cases, you should turn to any secondary legislation which is relevant. This law develops, codifies and expands the law but can only be produced by the EU institutions if related to a Treaty Article. The format of this secondary legislation is typically as regulations or as directives.

You should then familiarise your self with any cases which interpret and explain the provisions of this secondary legislation in the same way that you did for those cases relating to Articles above.

In this way, a 'paper trail' should develop which you can use to plot your way through each topic:

Article
Regulation or Directive
Supporting cases.

If you remember to do this and construct your study notes accordingly, it is hard to go wrong.

Guide to Using the Book and the Companion Website

The Routledge *Optimize* revision series is designed to provide students with a clear overview of the core topics in their course, and to contextualise this overview within a narrative that offers straightforward, practical advice relating to assessment.

Revision objectives

These overviews are a brief introduction of the core themes and issues you will encounter in each chapter.

Chapter Topic Maps

Visually link together all of the key topics in each chapter to tie together understanding of key issues.

Illustrative diagrams

A series of diagrams and tables are used to help facilitate the understanding of concepts and interrelationships within key topics.

Up for Debate

Up for debate features help you to critique current law and reflect on how and in which direction it may develop in the future.

Case precedent boxes

A variety of landmark cases are highlighted in text boxes for ease of reference. The facts, principle and application for the case are presented to help understand how these courses are used in legal problems.

Aim Higher and Common Pitfalls

These assessment focused sections show students how to get the best marks, and avoid the most common mistakes.

Table of key cases

Drawing together all of the key cases from each chapter

Companion Website

www.routledge.com/revision

Visit the Law Revision website to discover a comprehensive range of resources designed to enhance your learning experience.

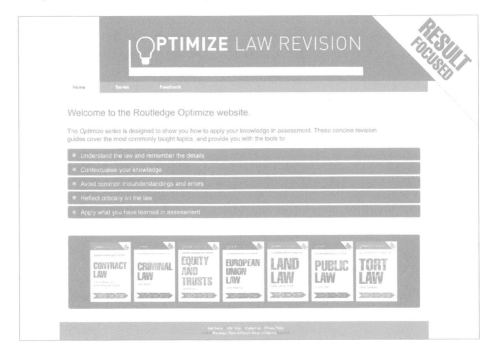

Resources for Optimize Law revision

- ❖ Revision tips podcasts
- ❖ Topic overview podcasts
- ❖ Subject maps for each topic
- ❖ Downloadable versions of Chapter Maps and other diagrams
- ❖ Flashcard Glossary
- ❖ MCQ questions

Table of Cases and Statutes

■ Cases

▉ Statutes and EU Legislation

1

The EU: History, Institutions and Sources of Law

Revision objectives

Understand the law
- Do you understand the formation and driving principles behind the EU?

Remember the details
- Can you explain the significance of the different treaties?

Reflect critically on areas of debate
- Do you understand how the institutions work together and their respective roles?

Contextualise
- Can you see how this foundation chapter sets up the subsequent topics?

Apply your skills and knowledge
- Could you explain the development and legal standing of the EU?

Chapter Map

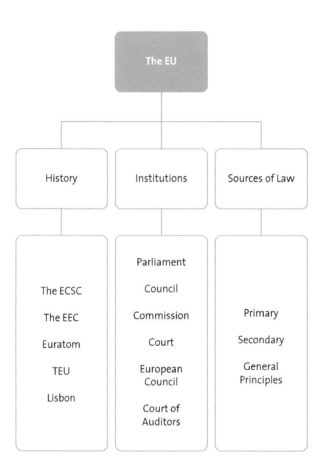

History of the EU

Introduction

At the conclusion of the Second World War with Europe in a state of economic, political and moral turmoil, it was clear that a pathway was needed for reconstruction and co-operation between the European states. The first step was the Council of Europe formed in 1949 for closer political integration.

However, in economic terms, it was from the Schuman Plan that the current European Union developed.

The *Schuman Plan* envisaged the merging of production of what, at that time, were the two wartime necessities, coal and steel, to ensure these could not be used to promote war. With this in mind, it proposed that the control of these sections of the economy was given over to an independent international authority, the High Authority, comprising individuals who were not government representatives but who were given the power to fix prices and ensure compliance with competition rules.

The Schuman experiment in economic cooperation involved the removal of these vital wartime industries from the control of the national governments in the hope of providing a surer foundation for peace and stability in Europe.

While the original plan (drafted by French statesman Jean Monnet and the French Foreign Minister Robert Schuman) only envisaged France and Germany acceding to this Treaty, Schuman invited the rest of Western Europe to join.

In the resulting conference (1950) France, Germany, Italy and the Benelux nations produced the draft treaty (1951) that created the European Coal and Steel Community (ECSC).

Significantly, the Treaty aimed at a federal Europe.

The beginning

Following these early steps, the EU was created as outlined below:

| 1951 | | Treaty of Paris | | European Coal and Steel Community (ECSC) |

All trade barriers in coal and steel had to be removed, trade was expanded and the High Authority established a common pricing policy and production limits rationalising production

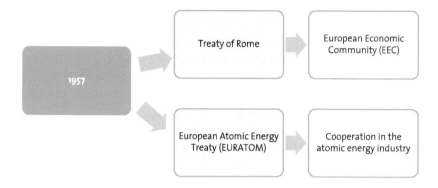

The next step

However, the ambitions of the Member States did not stop there and the EU really came into being following the Maastricht reforms and innovations in 1992.

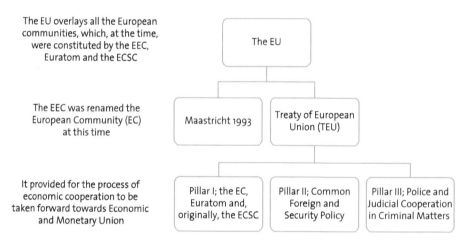

Foundations of the EU

These four treaties, the ECSC Treaty, the Euratom Treaty, the EC Treaty and the TEU, are the founding treaties of the EU.

The amending treaties

As noted in the preface, EU law is civil law and advanced through a sequence of further, amending treaties:

1965 The Merger Treaty

❖ The institutions of the then existing three European communities, the ECSC, the EEC and Euratom, were merged into a common Commission and Council of Ministers in addition to the already shared Assembly and Court of Justice.

1986 The Single European Act (SEA)	❖ It increased the areas of EEC competence, provided for democratic and institutional changes designed to make the communities more accountable and efficient and laid the foundation for the completion of the internal market. ❖ The Assembly was also officially renamed the European Parliament (EP) and the Court of First Instance (CFI) was established.
1997 Treaty of Amsterdam (TEA)	❖ A consolidating treaty, it sought to improve decision-making processes and to make the existing treaty structure more comprehensible.
2001 Treaty of Nice	❖ Entering into force in 2003, the focus of the ToN was on preparing the ground for the substantial enlargement of the EU through the accession of ten new Member States, primarily from Eastern and Central Europe, which went ahead in May 2004.

The accession treaties

The accession treaties are the treaties through which new Member States join the communities and the Union. The EU is now comprised of 28 Member States.

1957	❖ France, Germany, Italy, the Netherlands, Belgium and Luxembourg
1973	❖ Denmark, Ireland and the UK
1981	❖ Greece
1986	❖ Spain and Portugal
1995	❖ Austria, Sweden and Finland
2004	❖ The Czech Republic, Slovakia, Slovenia, Poland, Lithuania, Latvia, Estonia, Hungary, Cyprus and Malta
2007	❖ Bulgaria and Romania
2013	❖ Croatia

The Lisbon treaty

One of the aims of the Lisbon Treaty was to merge the three pillars of the EU into a single structure with simpler and more transparent decision-making processes. The Treaty was not intended substantially to alter how the EU works, its institutional structure or the range of areas of competence in which the EU can act.

Euratom remains a separate entity, but, otherwise, the original Treaties have been replaced by the Lisbon Treaty. Integrated into this is the Charter of Fundamental Rights, which contains the rights and principles that the EU and its Member States must respect when making or giving effect to European law.

Under Lisbon, the distribution of powers, or competences as they are called, between the Member States and EU, the principles, such as subsidiarity and proportionality, which govern the exercise of power by the EU and the types of acts through which it can exercise power are consolidated, clarified and simplified.

A similar rationalisation is undertaken in relation to the institutional framework. Most importantly, the European Council is established directly under the Treaty as a full institution with a permanent President and the position of European Foreign Minister is created. Membership of the European Parliament is limited to 750 and the Commission (currently comprised of one Commissioner from each Member State) will be, ultimately, reduced to two-thirds of that size.

Provision is made for the increased influence of national parliaments in the making of EU legislation. Other changes include redefinition and extension of the current qualified majority voting system in the Council and general reliance on the co-decision procedure between the Parliament and the Council, which is called the 'ordinary legislative procedure' under the Treaty, in the making of EU legislation (qualified majority voting and the co-decision procedure are discussed in more detail in the next chapter). In more controversial areas, such as defence, increased cooperation is encouraged, but the processes of cooperation remain fundamentally in the hands of the Member States.

The main Treaty we are now concerned with is the Treaty of the European Union (TOTEU) and the Treaty on the Functioning of the European Union (TFEU). In reality, this comprises two separate treaties, but it is generally referred to as one document, reflecting the fact it emerged from one process (the Treaty of Lisbon).

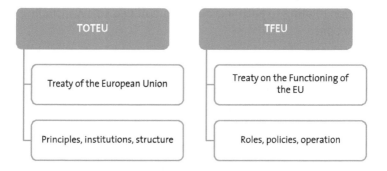

Institutions of the EU

The following section will outline and explain the key institutions of the EU. You will probably be familiar with many of these already.

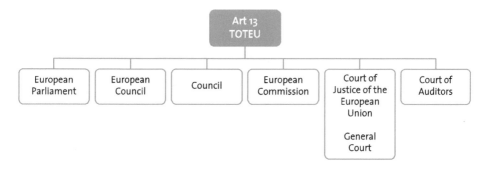

In addition, the EU institutions have a number of objectives which have been outlined in various treaty articles over the years. The current list is as follows:

Goals to be achieved
❖ Prohibition of customs duties between MS
❖ Common commercial policy
❖ Internal market where obstacles to free movement of goods, persons, services and capital are abolished
❖ Common agriculture and fisheries policy
❖ Systems ensuring competition is not distorted
❖ Approximation of the laws of the MS to ensure the proper functioning of the common market
❖ Non-discrimination and citizenship of the Union

Key information relating to each institution is outlined below including their main roles and functions.

The European Parliament

The key Articles relating to this body are in the centre of the following diagram which outlines the key information for the European Parliament:

Article 14 TOTEU Articles 223–234 TFEU

Location
- ❖ Strasbourg
- ❖ The EP's committees sit in Brussels and its secretariat is divided between Brussels and Luxembourg

Personnel
- ❖ The EP shall be composed of representatives of the Union's citizens
- ❖ MEPs are directly elected for five-year terms from each MS

Role
- ❖ The EP undertakes a range of legislative, budgetary and supervisory roles
- ❖ The extent of the EP's involvement in the legislative process depends on which procedure is required to adopt a Community measure in a particular subject area
- ❖ The co-decision procedure has been recognised as by far the most important, and is now referred to as the 'ordinary legislative procedure'

Functions
- ❖ The EP has approval powers over the whole of the EU budget. The process allows the EP to push for its own priorities to be reflected in the budget. The EP has the power to reject the budget in its entirety
- ❖ The EP also performs substantial supervisory functions

Thus, it is the case that the EP has a number of important functions but their supervisory role is key.

Supervisory functions of the EP
Power to set up a 'Committee of Inquiry' into allegations of maladministration
Receiving petitions from EU citizens on matters within the scope of Community activity affecting the individual directly

Appointing an Ombudsman to investigate disputes between citizens and the EU's administrative authorities
Submitting questions orally or in writing to the Commission to which the Commission is required to reply
Approval of a new Commission and its President
Debate of the Commission's Annual General Report
Power to pass a motion of censure of the Commission by a two-thirds majority vote, upon which the Commission is required to resign as a whole
Submitting questions orally or in writing to the Council
Standing to bring proceedings against another institution under Articles 263 and 265 TFEU
Power, under the assent procedure, to veto the accession of new Member States
Right to recourse to the CJ for annulment of acts adopted or failure of the Commission or Council to fulfil its obligations

The European Council

Article 15 TOTEU Articles 235–236 TFEU

History

❖ The European Council is not mentioned in the original founding treaties, despite the fact that summits did occur in the early years of the EEC
❖ The name 'European Council' was not used until the Paris Summit of 1974 and did not appear in a treaty until the SEA in 1986

Personnel

❖ The Heads of Government of the Member States and the President of the Commission
❖ The post of a stable presidency (Articles 15(5) and (6) TOTEU)
❖ This is a post now elected by the European Council itself, with a 30-month term of office
❖ Previously the Presidency rotated amongst the Member States every six months

Role

❖ The European Council shall provide the Union with the necessary impetus for its development and shall define the general political directions and priorities thereof

Functions

❖ Article 15(3) TOTEU requires that the European Council meets at least twice every six months

❖ It plays an enormously important role in taking long-term strategic decisions about the EU, so providing political direction for the continuing and future development of the Union
❖ It shall not exercise legislative functions (Article 15(1) TOTEU)

The Council (often referred to as the 'Council of Ministers')

Articles 237–243 TFEU

Location
❖ Brussels
❖ Subsidiary location in Luxembourg

Personnel
❖ The Council has a variable membership dependent on the subject matter under consideration, each member being a representative of his or her Member State at Ministerial level
❖ For instance, where the external relations of the EU are at issue, the Foreign Ministers of Member States will form the Council
❖ The Presidency of the Council is allotted by rotation (Article 16 TOTEU and Article 236 TFEU)

Role
❖ Council members are politically accountable to their national governments
❖ In contrast to the Commission, the Council represents the interests of Member States.

Functions
❖ The Council is the main decision-making body within the EU, having both executive and legislative powers, although some executive powers are devolved to the Commission and some legislative powers are shared with the Parliament under the 'ordinary legislative' (co-decision) procedure
❖ Together with the EP, it constitutes the budgetary authority to adopt the EU budget

The way in which legislation is produced in the EU is very complex and there are a number of different processes as outlined below.

These differ according to the area of law and involve collaboration between both institutions and Member States.

Decision-making procedures

There are a number of procedures through which legislation is made in the EU, generally involving some form of collaboration between the institutions with the Council playing a very important role.

Procedure	Advantages	Disadvantages
Simple Majority	A simple majority approach	This is rarely used to decide an issue, because to do so would see individual MS cede too much power to other MS in the decision-making process
Unanimity	This was the initially favoured method of decision making. It still remains in those areas of Union action where Member States are most concerned to protect national interests	However, unanimity is difficult to achieve, effectively allowing any single Member State to veto a Union proposal and so creating a decision-making process with a high degree of inbuilt inertia
Qualified Majority Voting (QMV)	QMV prevents any one MS, or even a small block of MS, from vetoing a decision being made	It is a complex system of weighted voting, which requires first that a certain number of the weighted votes be cast in favour of a decision for it to be adopted, but also that a majority of Member States vote in its favour representing a certain percentage of the EU population

By 2014 the position will be that a QMV comprises two elements:

At least 55% of EU States must agree (i.e. at 27, 15 Member States); and

States representing at least 65% of the EU's population must agree

The Commission: 'The guardian of the treaties'

Articles 244–250 TFEU

Location
* Brussels and has a subsidiary base in Luxembourg

Personnel
* It is comprised of one Commissioner from each Member State, up to a maximum of 28
* At present, there are 28 Commissioners, who are appointed for five-year terms and are 'chosen on the grounds of their general competence'
* Commission appointments need the approval of the EP and the Presidency is elected by the EP on the recommendation of the Council

Role
* The 'executive' of the EU (Article 17 TOTEU), being responsible for the initiation of Union policy in areas of Union competence and ensuring that policy is properly implemented
* The role of the Commission is not simply executive and it also performs important legislative and supervisory functions

Functions
* Legislative
* Budgetary
* Supervisory
* External Relations

This is arguably the most important EU institution as it is at the heart of the EU administration with an important role in creating and maintaining cohesiveness. The key functions are outlined as follows:

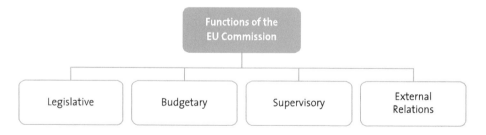

One of the key areas is the making of legislation in tandem with the other institutions.

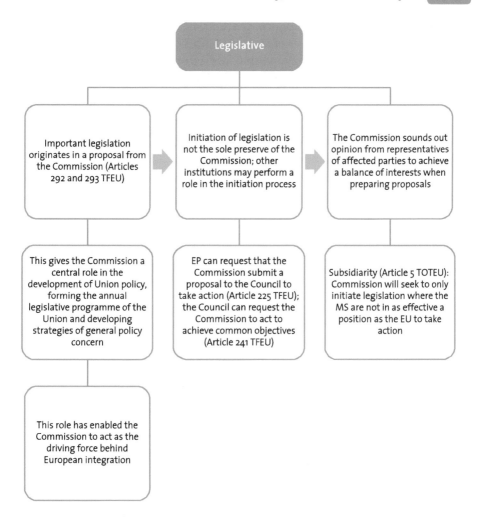

In addition, it is important that the Commission manages the EU finances and to this end, a budget must be constructed and be approved each year.

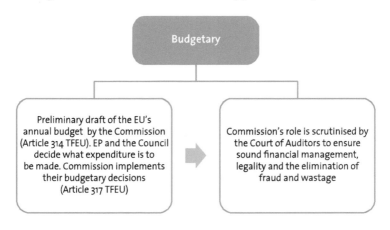

As noted in relation to the Council, the Commission also plays a major role in supervising both the behaviour of Member States to ensure that they are fulfilling their roles correctly and legally within the structure of the EU. Similarly, the Commission may take action against the other institutions. In this way, they inhabit their 'Guardian of the Treaties' role.

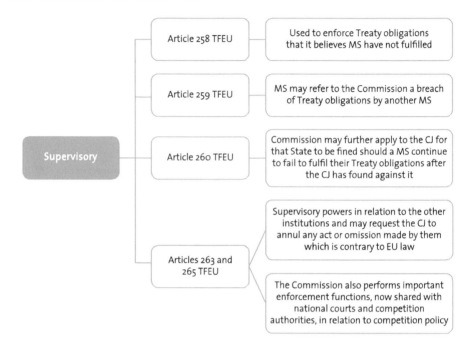

Finally, it is worth noting that the Commission has a further role in liasing with states outside the EU.

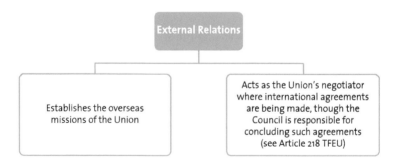

The Court of Justice of the European Union and the General Court

As students, it is this body and the decisions it makes which often receive the most attention.

Article 19 TOTEU Articles 251–281 TFEU

Location
- Luxembourg

Personnel
- 27 judges, one from each MS of recognised competence and independent
- Appointed for a renewable term of six years
- Appointments rotate on a three-year basis
- They choose one of their number to be President for a renewable term of three years
- Eight Advocates-General (AGs), who deliver in open court a reasoned and impartial opinion on most cases which go before the CJ
- The AG's opinion reviews both the facts and the parties' submissions before describing the appropriate law
- It has no legal force and it need not be followed by the CJ, though it may be highly influential and will often set out the facts and relevant law more clearly than the judgment of the Court

Role
- The CJ is the 'guardian of EU law' and has furthered the objectives of the founding treaties of the EU by taking into account the purposes underlying them in interpreting their meaning and giving effect to legislation made under them
- It has looked to the intention behind the words of the treaties, rather than interpreting them literally, so as to ensure the full effectiveness of EU law
- Under this approach, precedents may be applied and departed from much more flexibly than within the UK, where the courts have generally taken a more formal and rigid approach in interpreting and applying the law

Functions
- Judgments are by majority and collegiate. There is only one judgment and no dissenting opinions
- It may be heard in Full Court (a quorum of 15), which occurs only in the most exceptional cases, in a Grand Chamber (13 Judges) or in Chambers (three five judges)
- The CJ hears appeals from the General Court on points of law only (Article 256 TFEU)
- The CJ also has jurisdiction in disputes relating to the award of compensation for non-contractual damages (Articles 268 and 340 TFEU)

The court is able to play an important part in making sure that the laws of the EU are implemented properly throughout the Union and has the following enforcement mechanisms:

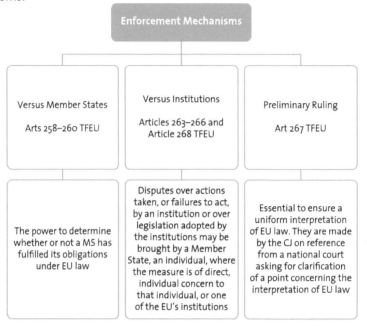

The General Court
This was originally called the Court of First Instance.

Arts 254–257 TFEU

History
* ❖ Formerly known as the Court of First Instance, the General Court is an independent Court attached to the CJ

Personnel
* ❖ Like the CJ, its membership comprises 27 Judges, one from each Member State, elected for six years by common accord of the Member States
* ❖ Again, like the CJ, the Judges of the General Court elect their own President

Role
* ❖ It was introduced by the SEA to ease the pressure of work on the CJ
* ❖ Operational from 1 November 1989

Functions

❖ It decides at first instance, with some exceptions, all direct actions brought by individuals against institutions of the EU, actions brought by MS against the Commission, actions seeking compensation for damage caused by institutions to their staff, actions relating to EU trademarks and appeals against decisions taken by the EU Civil Service Tribunal

❖ Appeals on points of law are heard in the CJEU

The Court of Auditors

Arts 285–287 TFEU

Location

❖ Luxembourg

Personnel

❖ 27 members, one from each Member State, chosen from amongst persons who have belonged to audit bodies in their own countries (or who are similarly qualified) and whose independence is 'beyond doubt'

❖ Members are appointed for six year terms

❖ The President is elected by the members of the Court for a renewable three-year term

Role

❖ To independently audit the revenue and spending of the Union and to certify that its accounts are legal and reliable

❖ The Court examines whether the Union's funds have been properly managed so as to ensure economy, efficiency and effectiveness

Functions

❖ It can be consulted by the Council and Parliament about the budget and its remit extends beyond the EU institutions to include any national, regional or local body that handles EU funds

❖ Its findings form part of the Court's Annual Report, which is published each November

❖ It is this Report that contains the 'statement of assurance' that good accounting practice has been followed and, as a result of sound practice, the financial objectives of the Union have been met

Sources of EU law

The sources split into primary and secondary as follows:

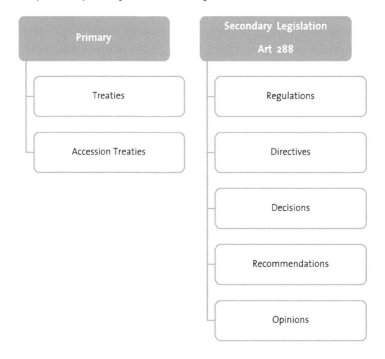

In addition, secondary legislation either has a binding or non-binding effect:

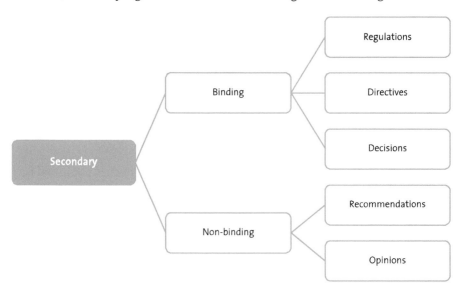

Secondary legislation: Key points

Regulations
- Apply and are binding throughout the EU
- Take immediate effect without requiring any further implementation by a MS
- 'Directly applicable': automatically become law within the MS

Directives
- Not directly applicable; do not automatically become law within the MS
- Sets out an objective which MS must seek to achieve and each MS has to decide how a particular directive is to be implemented or achieved
- Each MS has discretion as to the method it uses to implement a directive, directives are binding as to the result that must be achieved and specific deadlines for implementation are generally specified within directives

Decisions
- Decisions are binding on their addressees only; they do not require further implementation by MS
- Decisions may be addressed to MS collectively or singularly, or to individuals/undertakings

Recommendations and opinions
- Recommendations and opinions have no binding force and do not amount to legal decisions or acts. For this reason, they are often referred to as 'soft law'

General principles of EU law

The 'general principles' are the principles used, *inter alia*, by the CJ to interpret EU Law. They are specifically derived from the legal traditions and values common to all the Member States. The CJ has used them to determine cases and it views them as underlying the application of EU law.

The general principles may be used in the following ways:

Aid to interpretation

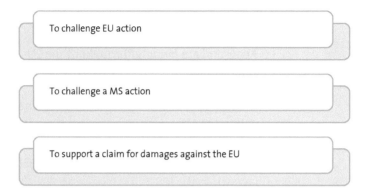

To challenge EU action

To challenge a MS action

To support a claim for damages against the EU

The following are examples of what have become accepted as the general principles:

General principles of EU law					
Equality	Legal certainty Legitimate expectation	Natural justice	Legal professional privilege	Proportionality	Human rights

Equality

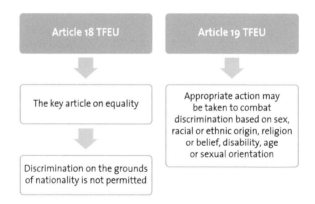

Article 18 TFEU

The key article on equality

Discrimination on the grounds of nationality is not permitted

Article 19 TFEU

Appropriate action may be taken to combat discrimination based on sex, racial or ethnic origin, religion or belief, disability, age or sexual orientation

Article 18 can be seen as the traditional EU approach which has the major focus on nationality. Article 19 represents a broader approach to discrimination which is more akin to the broader human rights objectives found in each Member State.

These are supported by a raft of other measures including Article 157 TFEU relating to discrimination based on gender.

Legal certainty and legitimate expectation

Case precedent – *CNTA v Commission*

Facts: Producers of Colza Oils, alleged, in support of an Article 340 TFEU (then Article 288 EC) action, that Regulation 189/72 was illegal. Regulation 189/72 discontinued compensation payments that had been made to those dealing in colza seeds. No warning had been given that this would be the effect of the Regulation. The company claimed that it had a legitimate expectation that compensatory amounts would be maintained for deliveries in progress. The Regulation had frustrated that expectation and caused extensive trading losses to CNTA.

Principle: The CJ held that by failing to provide a transitional measure in the Regulation, pursuant to which traders could have avoided such losses, the Commission had breached the general principle of legitimate expectation.

Application: This illustrates that, in producing new secondary legislation, the EU must be aware of already existing legal arrangements.

Legal certainty

- Prevents an EU measure (i.e. Treaty articles, regulations, directives and decisions) from taking effect from a point in time before its publication

Legitimate expectation

- One that may be held by a reasonable person with regard to events likely to occur in the normal cause of his/her affairs
- In the absence of an overriding matter of public interest, Union law must not violate the legitimate expectation of those affected by it

Natural justice: The right to a hearing

This subdivides into a number of heads which, in many respects, mirror, the heads of challenge under UK judicial review.

Case precedent – *Transocean Marine Paint Association v Commission*

Facts: This case concerns EU competition law (Articles 101 and 102 TFEU) and is dealt with in more detail in later chapters. TMPA took action to annul a decision of the Commission, which had been addressed to TMPA and which stated that TMPA's trading agreements were in breach of EU law.

Principle: The Court stated that it was a general rule that persons whose interests are perceptibly affected by a decision taken by a public authority must be given the opportunity to make their views known. Since the Commission had failed to comply with this obligation its decision was annulled.

Application: This is similar to the UK laws applying in administrative law and judicial review.

Legal professional privilege

Case precedent – *AM & S Ltd v Commission*

Facts: AM & S brought an action to annul a Commission decision. The Commission decision had required AM & S to produce various documents to assist a Commission investigation into suspected breaches of competition law. The company argued that it did not have to produce its communications with its lawyers, on the basis of legal professional privilege, a concept which it claimed was recognised in most Member States.

Principle: The CJ carried out a comparative survey and found that:

> ... provided that ... such communications are made for the purposes and in the interests of the client's rights of defence, and ... they emanate from independent lawyers, that is ... lawyers who are not bound to the client by ... employment then privilege will be recognized.

Application: Again, this is a principle that can be found in UK administrative law.

Proportionality

The concept of proportionality means that any measure taken by the Community must be proportionate to and suitable for the purposes which are to be achieved. No burden should be imposed on the citizen that is disproportionate to the objective of the measures. It is, in effect, a three-fold test:

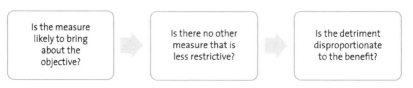

Is the measure likely to bring about the objective? → Is there no other measure that is less restrictive? → Is the detriment disproportionate to the benefit?

Case precedent – *Bela Mühle Josef Bergman KG v Grows-Farm GmbH & Co KG*

Facts: This concerned a scheme pursuant to which producers of animal feed were forced to use skimmed milk in their product rather than the cheaper soya, in order to reduce a surplus.

Principle: The Court held that the obligation to purchase the milk had imposed a disproportionate burden on the animal-feed producers and was unlawful because skimmed milk was three times more expensive than soya.

Application: The principle of proportionality was used to check a decision of Union institutions.

Fundamental human rights

The original treaties did not deal with human rights and, accordingly, the Union institutions were not bound by any principles of human rights. It was left to the CJ to develop jurisprudence in this area to ensure that EU law would be subject to similar review on the grounds of human rights as Member States were under their respective national law.

Treaty recognition: TEU

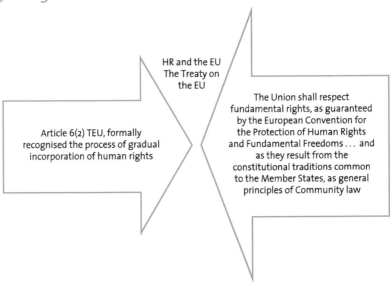

HR and the EU
The Treaty on
the EU

Article 6(2) TEU, formally recognised the process of gradual incorporation of human rights

The Union shall respect fundamental rights, as guaranteed by the European Convention for the Protection of Human Rights and Fundamental Freedoms ... and as they result from the constitutional traditions common to the Member States, as general principles of Community law

Treaty recognition: TOTEU

Article 6 TOTEU now incorporates the EU Charter of Fundamental Rights.

Note, however, that the UK has secured a Protocol (Protocol 30), attached to the treaty, which grants it a form of opt-out in regards to the Charter as below:

Article 1	Article 1
1. The Charter does not extend the ability of the CJEU or any court or tribunal of Poland or of the UK, to find that the laws . . . of Poland or of the UK are inconsistent with the fundamental rights, freedoms and principles that it reaffirms	. . . the Charter . . . shall only apply to Poland or the United Kingdom to the extent that the rights or principles that it contains are recognised in the law or practices of Poland or of the UK
2. Nothing in Title IV of the Charter creates justiciable rights applicable to Poland or the UK except in so far as Poland or the UK has provided for such rights in its national law	

Putting it into practice

'The EU is a fundamentally undemocratic and unaccountable entity.'

Critically discuss how far you agree with this statement.

Suggested solution

Introduction	• Use the essay title why would it be suggested that there are potential issues surrounding democracy and the EU perhaps a brief comparison with another state such as the UK would be useful.
Outline the EU structure	• Briefly explain each key institution and their respective roles in the EU. Make the point that unlike many EU states, the EU itself does not rely on separation of powers to ensure democracy it is a collaborative approach rather than a check and balance one.

Discuss and analyse the legislative process	• Show how the various legislative processes work and highlight the role of agreement and concensus in moving forward it is very difficult to introduce and gain approval for unpopular laws.

Outline accountability mechanisms	• As noted in Chapters 2, 3 and 4, there are various ways in which the EU, the institutions and the Member States themselves are accountable. This will highlight that the EU is accountable in many ways.

'The Democratic Deficit'	• This is the argument that the EU as an entity is too far removed from the citizens in each Member States who may argue that they have little say in the workings of the EU. This can be countered by highlighting some of the arguments above and by the recent trend in empowering MS through the concept of subsidiarity.

Conclusion	• From the above it should be clear that, despite the perception of the EU as lacking in democracy and accountability, there is enough evidence legally and politicallty to refute this.

Table of key cases referred to in this chapter

Case name	Area of law	Principle
AM & S Ltd v Commission C155/79 [1982] 2 CMLR 264	Legal professional privilege	Recognition that communications between clients and lawyers are protected.
Bela Mühle Josef Bergman KG v Grows-Farm GmbH & Co KG (the '*Skimmed Milk Powder*' case) C114/76 [1977] ECR 1211	Proportionality	An obligation to purchase the milk had imposed a disproportionate burden on the animal-feed producers and was unlawful because skimmed milk was three times more expensive than soya.

Case name	Area of law	Principle
CNTA v Commission C74/74 [1976] ECR 797	Legal certainty and legitimate expectation	The Commission did not produce a transitional measure thereby breaching this principle.
Transocean Marine Paint Association v Commission C17/74 [1974] ECR 1063	Natural justice: The right to a hearing	The Court stated that it was a general rule that persons whose interests are perceptibly affected by a decision taken by a public authority must be given the opportunity to make their views known. Since the Commission had failed to comply with this obligation its decision was annulled.

@ Visit the book's companion website to test your knowledge

❖ Resources include a subject map, revision tip podcasts, downloadable diagrams, MCQ quizzes for each chapter, and a flashcard glossary

❖ www.routledge.com/cw/optimizelawrevision

Revision objectives

Understand the law

- Do you understand the concept of enforcement and preliminary rulings?

Remember the details

- Can you explain the different types of enforcement mechanisms, the key Articles and supporting rules?

Reflect critically on areas of debate

- Do you understand the need for such mechanisms and their importance to the concept of EU harmony?

Contextualise

- Can you see how the concepts outlined in this chapter underpin the concepts of EU supremacy and the harmonisation of EU law?

Apply your skills and knowledge

- Can you explain and analyse this material in an essay on the need for such mechanisms?

Chapter Map

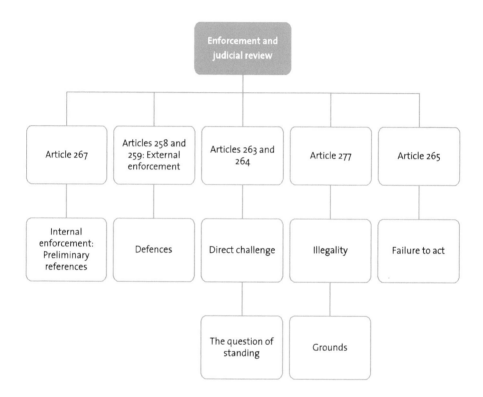

Introduction

Although most actions involving a Member State will now commence as a result of a direct effect, indirect effect or state liability action, it is also the case that cases can be brought against the government of a Member State directly before the CJ. There are various administrative and legal mechanisms which provide a number of pathways.

Internal enforcement: Article 267 TFEU

This refers to an action which originates from within the Member State itself as the result of a case starting in a court or tribunal of the state. The key legislation is Article 267.

Preliminary reference procedure

In this instance, a question raised in the domestic court can be referred to the Court of Justice (CJ) for an opinion. This generally occurs with a new piece of legislation or following the introduction of a new treaty when the bare law contained within has not yet been the subject of interpretation or application in the courts. Under the preliminary reference procedure, it is the national court that decides which specific issues should be referred to the CJ. After reaching its decision, the CJ returns the case to the national court which then makes the final decision. Cases can be referred to answer issues arising from the following:

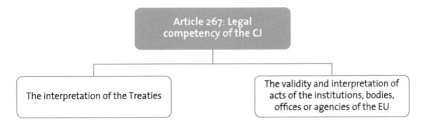

The way this procedure works in practice can be outlined as follows:

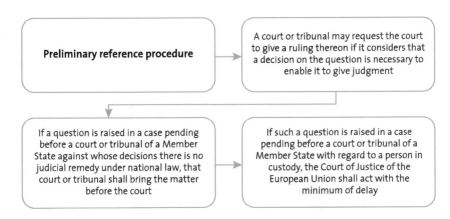

Aim Higher

Consider how many of the cases you will study in EU law began as preliminary references using this procedure. It is worth noting that key developments such as direct effect or state liability resulted from such actions.

Supplementary rules

The CJEU has also developed some important rules for determining whether such an action can be brought. These focus on the nature of the body in which the action is started and also deal with the question of whether such a reference is actually necessary. This is known as the *acte clair* doctrine:

Court or Tribunal
- ❖ *Garofalo*
- ❖ Must be established by law; permanent; its jurisdiction should be compulsory; its procedure should be inter-party; it should apply the rule of law; and it should be independent.

Acte Clair
- ❖ *Rheinmulhen*
- ❖ A court that has the power to make a preliminary reference can only do so if a question of EU law is raised and 'it considers that a decision on the question is necessary to enable it to give judgment'. The treaty therefore makes it clear that national courts have discretion as to whether or not to make a referral to the CJ.

Effect of preliminary rulings

After the CJ has reached its decision, that decision is then handed down to the national court that made the preliminary reference.

The national court is not obliged to apply the decision of the CJ, as it may decide the case on other grounds. However, if it does apply the decision of the CJ, it is bound by that ruling.

If the same issue arises again in a later case, whether in the courts of the same or a different Member State, the CJ may apply the same ruling. However, national courts are not precluded from making new preliminary references. They can do so if, for example, they consider that the previous ruling of the CJ is mistaken and want it to reconsider its position.

Unless a new preliminary reference is made, all of the national courts in the Member States should obey the decision of the CJ. It would be improper for a national court to depart from the CJ's decision simply because it considered it to be wrong.

External enforcement: Articles 258 and 259 TFEU

This refers to actions against Member States which start externally to the state at Member State or institution level. There are two key articles:

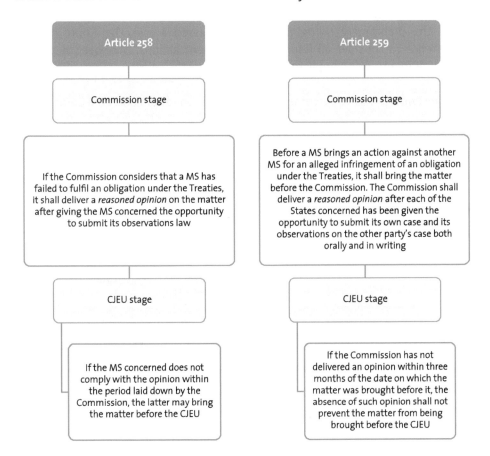

The reasoned opinion of the Commission

A 'reasoned opinion' formally records a violation committed by a Member State.

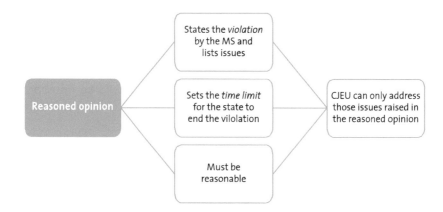

The role of the court in enforcement actions

Unlike the preliminary ruling procedure discussed above, the Court has full competence to consider all issues in enforcement actions. Moreover, it delivers actual judgments which apply to the matter before the court.

There are two alternative outcomes following a reasoned opinion by the Commission:

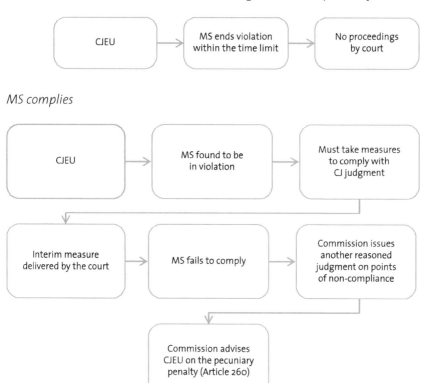

MS complies

MS fails to comply

Defences available to the MS		
Defence	Administrative difficulty/economic problems	The EU law is illegal	*Force majeure* (unforseen 'Act of God')
Case examples	*Commission v Belgium*	*BASF*	*Commission v Italy*
Principle and application	The Belgian Government pleaded that the complexity of construction works at the water station in a Belgian town meant that the authorities needed a longer time to comply with the European norm. However, this argument did not succeed in the court as it was made four years after the implementation date had passed – far too long!	The court does not usually accept this argument unless the relevant law concerned is so defective as to be deemed non-existent as in this case	The Italian Government failed to compile statistical returns according to Community Directive 78/546. The court accepted the *force majeure* defence as the Italian Data Processing Centre had suffered a bomb attack in 1978 and its vehicle register had been destroyed

Direct challenge to the legality of Community Acts: Article 263 TFEU

Article 263 TFEU

'The Court of Justice of the European Union shall review the legality of legislative acts, of acts of the Council, of the Commission and of the European Central Bank, other than recommendations and opinions, and of acts of the European Parliament and of the European Council intended to produce legal effects vis-à-vis third parties. It shall also review the legality of acts of bodies, offices or agencies of the Union intended to produce legal effects vis-à-vis third parties.'

This Article is the process for effective judicial review of the law and decisions produced by the EU itself.

A reviewable act will have legal effect until the act is set aside by the CJEU, under Article 264 which is outlined below:

Article 263	Article 264
• Proceedings should be started within two months of the publication of such a decision.	• If the action is well founded 'the Court of Justice shall declare the act concerned to be void'.

Who can bring an action?

In the UK, judicial review and human rights actions always have a preliminary stage whereby the legal standing of the applicant to bring the case is ascertained. This is also the case in the EU. The question is determined as follows:

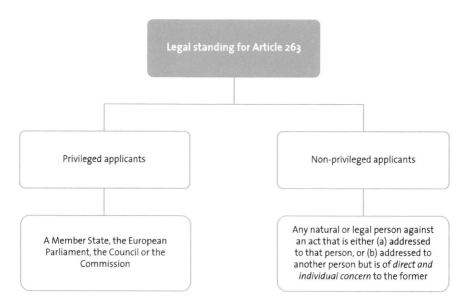

What does 'direct and individual concern' mean?

The CJEU has developed a filter system so that only mean' applicants connected in some way to the decision can actually challenge it – this is the direct and individual concern concept.

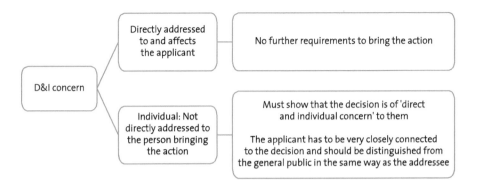

Case precedent – *Plaumann*

Facts: A trader in clementines, could not challenge the Commission's decision regarding the collection of duties on the importation of clementines from non-EU countries.

Principle: The court came up with the so-called 'closed category test'. It held that 'to establish individual concern the applicant must show that the measure affects him by reason of certain attributes peculiar to him or by reason of circumstances that differentiate him from all other persons just as in the case of the persons directly addressed'.

The court went on to say that a closed category is one in which the membership is fixed at the time of the decision, whereas an open category is one in which membership is not fixed at the time of the decision and anyone can enter it.

Plaumann was not a member of a closed group as anyone could join the trade.

Application: The 'closed category' test has been widely criticised for its restrictive effect. It has, in effect, prevented all direct actions being brought by private parties to challenge decisions that are addressed to others.

Plea for illegality and grounds for review: Article 277 TFEU

Article 277

'Notwithstanding the expiry of the period laid down in Article 263, sixth paragraph, any party may, in proceedings in which an act of general application adopted by an institution, body, office or agency of the Union is at issue, plead the grounds specified in Article 263, second paragraph, in order to invoke before the Court of Justice of the European Union the inapplicability of that act.'

Article 277 is not an independent cause of action, but an additional and incidental form of challenge that can be brought in an annulment action under Article 263. It is subject to two constraints. It cannot be used where the measure is already being challenged before a court elsewhere by the parties and it also cannot be used where the parties have already had the opportunity to challenge the measure but did not take up that opportunity.

If an applicant has overcome all of the procedural hurdles, they must convince the court that the measure needs to be annulled. One of the four broad grounds for review that are set out in Article 263 TFEU need to apply. These are outlined below.

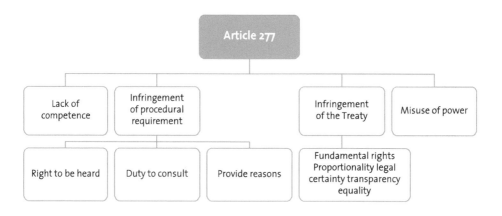

Lack of competence

This ground of review corresponds to substantive *ultra vires* in English law. EU institutions can only exercise the powers allocated to them by the Treaty and cannot assume new ones.

Case precedent – *France v Commission*

Facts: The Commission had concluded an agreement with the United States to lessen the possibility of conflict on the application of competition rules.

Principle: The court ruled that, under what is now Article 260 TFEU, the Commission had the power to negotiate agreements with States outside of the Community and international organisations, but that such agreements had to be concluded by the Council

Application: Although France succeeded in their challenge in this case, the ground is not used often due to the broad nature of the decision-making powers granted to the EU institutions by the Treaties.

Infringement of an essential procedural requirement

Infringement of an essential procedural requirement is one of the most popular grounds for review and is equivalent procedural *ultra vires* in English law. It comprises breaches of formal requirements contained in the Treaty and informal rules of fairness that are required by the General Principles of Community Law.

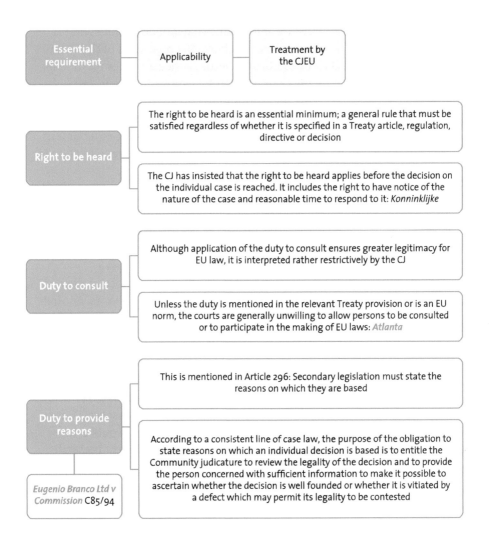

Essential requirement	Applicability	Treatment by the CJEU

Right to be heard

The right to be heard is an essential minimum; a general rule that must be satisfied regardless of whether it is specified in a Treaty article, regulation, directive or decision

The CJ has insisted that the right to be heard applies before the decision on the individual case is reached. It includes the right to have notice of the nature of the case and reasonable time to respond to it: *Konninklijke*

Duty to consult

Although application of the duty to consult ensures greater legitimacy for EU law, it is interpreted rather restrictively by the CJ

Unless the duty is mentioned in the relevant Treaty provision or is an EU norm, the courts are generally unwilling to allow persons to be consulted or to participate in the making of EU laws: *Atlanta*

Duty to provide reasons

This is mentioned in Article 296: Secondary legislation must state the reasons on which they are based

Eugenio Branco Ltd v Commission C85/94

According to a consistent line of case law, the purpose of the obligation to state reasons on which an individual decision is based is to entitle the Community judicature to review the legality of the decision and to provide the person concerned with sufficient information to make it possible to ascertain whether the decision is well founded or whether it is vitiated by a defect which may permit its legality to be contested

Infringement of the Treaty or any rule relating to its application

Through this ground the CJ has been able to use General Principles of Community law, such as non-discrimination, human rights, the rule of law, proportionality, etc to review the legality of EU legislation.

Fundamental rights	❖ MS legal systems and international law recognise that protection of fundamental rights may not be absolute at all times. However, any interference or limitations should be kept to a minimum.
Proportionality	❖ Article 5 TOTEU provides that the Union shall only act within the powers conferred on it by the Treaty and actions shall not go beyond what is necessary to achieve the objectives of the Treaty. To establish whether a measure is proportionate the Court usually asks three questions: (a) was the measure suitable to achieve the desired end; (b) was it necessary to achieve the desired end; and (c) whether the measure imposed a burden on the individual that was excessive in relation to the objective to be achieved.
Legal certainty	❖ This is part of the EU commitment to the Rule of Law. This principle takes on many legal forms. For instance, it can be used as a prohibition of retrospectivity – no rule should apply retrospectively to a situation that occurred prior to the date on which any given rule was. Another aspect of the principle of legal certainty is the protection of legitimate expectations, in which it is connected with the notion of 'good faith'.
Transparency	❖ Transparency has been a widely debated principle of EU law. It encompasses several aspects: access to documents, holding meetings in public, the provision of information, etc. Some of these are enshrined in the text of the TFEU; for example access to documents is set out in Article 215 TFEU, whilst others have been developed by the CJ.
Equality and non-discrimination	❖ The equality principle can be found in various provisions of the TFEU. Article 18 TFEU contains the general principle of non-discrimination.

Misuse of power

Misuse of power means that a measure has been adopted for the purposes other than those for which it was intended and corresponds to improper purpose in English administrative law.

Since the court requires 'objective, relevant and consistent indications of misuse of power' there are very few cases in which applicants have successfully claimed this ground.

Those few cases that exist usually tend to deal with staff of the European institutions (e.g. *Gutmann v Commission*).

Actions for failure to Act: Article 265 TFEU

Community institutions may breach the rules not only by exceeding their powers, but also by failing to carry out the duty imposed on them by the Treaty or some other provision having legal effect. This form of breach may result in action under

Article 265 TFEU

'Should the European Parliament, the European Council, the Council, the Commission or the European Central Bank, in infringement of the Treaties, fail to act, the Member States and the other institutions of the Union may bring an action before the Court of Justice of the European Union to have the infringement established. This Article shall apply, under the same conditions, to bodies, offices and agencies of the Union which fail to act.'

The action shall be admissible only if the institution, body, office or agency concerned has first been called upon to act. If, within two months of being so called upon, the institution, body, office or agency concerned has not defined its position, the action may be brought within a further period of two months.

Any natural or legal person may, under the conditions laid down in the preceding paragraphs, complain to the Court that an institution, body, office or agency of the Union has failed to address to that person any act other than a recommendation or an opinion.

Case precedent – *Ladbroke Racing (Deutschland) GmbH v Commission*

Facts: Ladbroke had complained to the Commission about the denial of access for the televising of horse racing, alleging breach of Articles 101 and 102 by the German and French companies in the horse racing and communications business.

After deciding to investigate the complaint in 1990, by 1992, the Commission had still not defined its position.

Principle: The CFI (now the General Court) found that the Commission should either have formulated its position on the alleged breach of Article 102, dismissed the complaint in a formal letter to the complainant, or made the reasoned decision not to pursue the complaint on the ground of the lack of Community interest. Lack of any decision constituted a ground for an Article 265 TFEU procedure.

Application: This illustrates how the EU processes can operate to punish a failure to act on the part of one of its institutions.

The Treaty does not specifically set a time limit within which EU institutions have to respond before a procedure for failure to act can be triggered against them. The court states that an Article 265 procedure should be initiated within a 'reasonable time'.

Usually once the request to act has been made the institution has two months within which to define its position. If it has not done this, the applicant has a further two months within which to bring an Article 265 action.

Putting it into practice

'Without doubt, the preliminary reference is the most valuable way to ensure both the accountability of Member States and the development of the law of the EU.'

How far do you agree with this statement?

Suggested solution

A very simple and commonly used technique is to outline the arguments in favour of and against the proposition. Again, the essay should be top and tailed with an introduction and a conclusion.

You should also outline how the Article 267 operates.

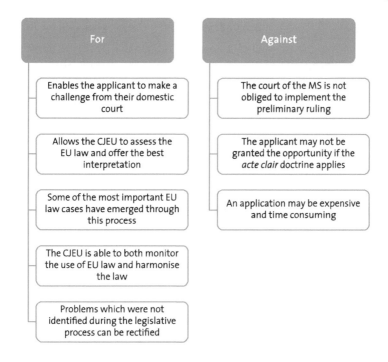

Conclusion

As can be seen, the evidence is pointing to support the proposition in the essay title.

Table of key cases referred to in this chapter

Case name	Area of law	Principle
Atlanta C104/9 [1995] ECR I-3761	Duty to consult	Unless this is specifically stated, the courts do not regard this as a given right.
BASF C137/92P [1994] ECR I-2555	Defences under Article 258	The EU law was so defective it was regarded as illegal.
Commission v Belgium C42/89 [1989] ECR I-3083	Defences under Article 258	The administrative difficulties cited by the Belgian Government were out of date.
Commission v Italy C101/84 [1985] ECR 2629	Defences under Article 258	The ECJ accepted a plea of *force majeure*.

Case name	Area of law	Principle
Eugenio Branco Ltd v Commission C85/94 [1995] ECR II-2555	Duty to provide reasons	This is to allow the applicant to judge whether an application is worth pursuing.
France v Commission C327/91 ECR I-3641	Lack of competence	A ruling on the legal powers of the Commission to conclude agreements outside the EU.
Garofalo C-69-79/96 [1997] ECR I-5603	Court or Tribunal	Established the rules for ascertaining the legal nature of the decision-making body.
Gutmann v Commission C18 and 35/65 [1966] ECR 103	Misuse of power	Usually applicable to staff of the EU institutions.
Konninklijke C48 and 66/90 ECR 1992 I-565	Right to be heard	This includes the right to have a reasonable period of time within which to respond.
Ladbroke Racing (Deutschland) GmbH v Commission (C74/92) [1998] ECR II-1	Article 265	The Commission failed to act allowing Ladbrokes to bring a case against them.
Plaumann v Commission C25/62 [1963] ECR 95	Direct and individual concern	The court introduced the 'closed-category' test.

@ **Visit the book's companion website to test your knowledge**

❖ Resources include a subject map, revision tip podcasts, downloadable diagrams, MCQ quizzes for each chapter, and a flashcard glossary
❖ www.routledge.com/cw/optimizelawrevision

3

European Law Supremacy and Direct Effect

Revision objectives

Understand the law
- Can you outline the concepts of EU supremacy and the doctrine of direct effect?
- How did these concepts develop?

Remember the details
- Can you remember the tests for direct effect for Treaty Articles, Regulations and Directives?
- Can you define each element of the direct effect tests with case law examples?

Reflect critically on areas of debate
- Do you understand how a directive differs in relation to direct effect?
- Can you define the concept of state emanation accurately and critically discuss in relation to case law examples?

Contextualise
- Can you relate these concepts to other areas of EU law such as the free movement issues?

Apply your skills and knowledge
- Could you complete an essay and problem question in this area?

Chapter Map

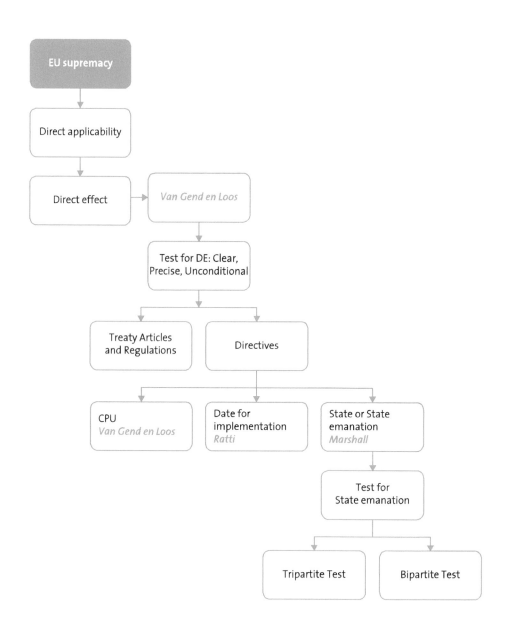

Introduction – What is EU supremacy?

The CJEU (ECJ) states that Community law is supreme over all national law and that Member States should not produce legislation which would conflict with EU law.

Case precedent – *Costa v ENEL*

Facts: Mr Costa challenged his electricity bill.

The integration into the laws of each MS of provisions which derive from the Community, and more generally the terms and spirit of the Treaty, make it impossible for the States . . . to accord precedence to a unilateral and subsequent measure over a legal system accepted by them on the basis of reciprocity.

Principle: EU Supremacy.

Application: Laws produced by Member States can be challenged on the ground that they contravene EU law.

What is direct effect?

This new concept was introduced in 1962 in the case *Van Gend en Loos*. It allows individuals to bring actions using EU law in their national courts thereby giving these rights 'direct effect'.

Permitting the people and national courts of the Member States into the process of enforcing the EU law in this way made it much more likely that the obligations on Member States under the Treaty would be upheld.

With this development, not only did the Commission and Member States have authority to seek to enforce those obligations, but also the citizens of Member States. As such, the decision took a giant step towards achieving integration, uniformity and effectiveness in the application of EU law within the national legal systems of Member States.

Case precedent – *Van Gend en Loos*

Facts: *Van Gend en Loos* imported urea formaldehyde from West Germany into Holland in 1960. Because of changes to the classification of this product by the Dutch authorities, the duty payable on it had been increased from 3% to 8%. However, Article 12 EEC (now see Article 30 TFEU) provided at the time there should be no new customs duties between Member States. *Van Gend en Loos* argued before the Dutch authorities that Article 12 (now Article 30 TFEU) gave rise to rights which could be claimed by individuals and protected in the courts of Member States and that the company had an enforceable claim because the increased duty was contrary to Article 12. On a reference to the CJ from the Dutch Customs Court, the CJ held that Article 12 was enforceable in national courts.

Principle: Direct effect.

Application: To allow individuals to use EU law in their national state.

Van Gend en Loos is an illustration of the CJ filling in the gaps left in the 'framework treaty' that was the EC Treaty. The Treaty established the structure for Member State cooperation and sets out in broad terms certain objectives and rights and obligations. The detail has in many respects been provided by the CJ through the kind of purposive interpretation of the Treaty that characterised its judgment in *Van Gend en Loos.*

Aim Higher

As you progress through this chapter, think about how these concepts relate to the substantive areas of EU law such as Free Movement of Persons. For example, without the establishment of the concept of direct effect it would not have been possible for individuals to complain about discrimination in their national courts. This is a foundation area so a strong appreciation of this will help you in understanding how many of the main EU topics have been advanced through the courts.

However, before proceeding it is worth defining another concept which can be the source of some confusion in this area: the meaning of direct applicability.

Article 288 TFEU specifies the forms of secondary legislation that the institutions of the Community must use to fulfil the objects of the Treaty. Of those, a regulation is described as being of 'general application ... binding in its entirety and *directly applicable* in all Member States' (emphasis added).

What direct applicability means in this context is that once a regulation is made by the Community it does not need to be transposed into the domestic law of Member States; it automatically becomes part of their domestic law.

This is to be contrasted with the effect of directives, which, while also binding, are described in Article 288 as binding only 'as to the result to be achieved', leaving to Member States the 'form and method' of their achievement. Consequently, directives require Member States to take national measures to transpose the terms of a directive into their domestic law. Therefore, unlike regulations, they are not directly applicable.

Direct effect refers to the fact that provisions of EU law may, even without transposition by a Member State, give rise to rights which can be enforced by individuals within the national legal systems of Member States. Such rights arise where the conditions for direct effect are satisfied (these conditions are discussed below).

Direct applicability	Direct effect
❖ Directly applicable: ❖ 'shall have general application, shall be binding in . . . entirety and directly applicable in all member states'; ❖ needs no additional measures.	❖ Directly effective: ❖ confers immediate *rights* on individuals; ❖ applied even if conflicts with national laws

The application of *Van Gend en Loos*

For a provision of EU law to be directly effective, certain criteria must be satisfied. Two basic requirements for a provision of Community law to be directly effective that have evolved from this. The first is that the provision must be sufficiently clear and precise to give rise to an identifiable individual right (or rights). The second is that it must be unconditional. A provision which satisfies the *Van Gend en Loos* criteria is 'legally complete and consequently capable of producing direct effects' (*Costa v ENEL*).

Case precedent – *Defrenne v SABENA (No 2)*

Facts: Defrenne claimed she had suffered sex discrimination as a female worker in terms of pay as compared with male 'cabin stewards' who did the same work. Both parties to the action accepted that there had been discrimination, but whether Defrenne had any legal right to be protected against such discrimination under EU law was the key question. The Court held that Article 119 (now Article 157 TFEU) could give rise to rights which protected against direct discrimination where a person by virtue of their gender received less pay than a person of the other gender for the same work, as had occurred in Defrenne's case.

Principle: Direct effect and the *Van Gend* criteria.

Application: The Treaty article was sufficiently clear and precise and unconditional to provide such a right.

What about positive obligations to act?

Van Gend en Loos left unanswered the question of whether Treaty articles which imposed a positive obligation could be directly effective. Such articles are more problematical from a direct effect perspective as a positive obligation appears on its face to be necessarily conditional, as it requires Member States to do something to give effect to the protected principle.

This question was answered in the following case.

Case precedent – *Alfons Lütticke GmbH v Hauptzollamt Saarlouis*

Facts: This concerned the scope of Article 95 (now Article 110 TFEU). Article 110 includes a prohibition on Member States introducing internal taxation measures which discriminate against the goods of other Member States. However, at the time the Treaty was first agreed to, it also imposed a positive obligation on Member States to remove, by 1 January 1962, any existing measures which had such a discriminatory effect.

The CJ held that there was no discretion left to Member States to give effect to the positive obligation regarding removal of discriminatory internal taxes once the 1 January 1962 deadline had passed. At this point the provision became directly effective.

Principle: Positive direct effect.

Application: To compel Member States to act positively to provide rights for their citizens.

The problem with directives

Directives are addressed to each Member State and, unless implemented by the Member State, they cannot be used in an action by one individual against another. That is, they can only be used vertically, not horizontally.

Treaty Articles and Regulations	Directives
❖ Are directly applicable. ❖ Have DE if they satisfy the VGL criteria. They can be used vertically (versus state) or horizontally (versus individual).	❖ Do not work in the same way. ❖ Addressed to Member State to achieve a particular objective/purpose. ❖ State chooses legal method for implementation. ❖ Only work vertically, not horizonrtally.

Aim Higher

Consider the different legal impact of directives versus regulations. Why does the EU choose one over the other and why should directives not have horizontal effect?

Consider the comments in *Marshall* in more detail. It would be helpful to understand why the court has taken this approach in expanding the notion of the state. The expansion of the concept of the emanation allows for a fairer approach without taking away the essential fact that directives can only be vertically directly effective.

Why? The answer relates to the fact that the failure to implement the statute lies with the Member State, not the individual who should not therefore be liable in relation to the state's failure to fulfil their EU duty and implement the directive.

Case precedent – *Marshall v Southampton and South West Area Health Authority (Teaching) (No. 1)*

Facts: This concerned a female dietician, who was dismissed on the ground that she had passed the compulsory retiring age applicable to women. Female employees were required to retire at 60, whereas male employees could continue to work until they were 65.

Marshall, who was then 62, complained that her dismissal violated Directive 76/207, the Equal Treatment Directive, which prohibited discrimination in working conditions on the grounds of sex.

The CJ held that the Directive was directly effective against the state and that Marshall could rely upon it in her claim against Southampton Health Authority. The health authority was an 'organ' of the state (what is now referred to as 'an emanation of the state') and so a part of the state. The fact that the authority was acting in its capacity as an employer rather than a public authority made no difference. *An individual relying on a directive against the state may do so whatever capacity it is acting in*. As to the rules on compulsory retirement, they were discriminatory and in breach of the Directive. The Court rejected the horizontal effect of directives.

Principle: The vertical effect *only* of directives.

Application: An individual cannot bring a action based on an unimplemented directive versus another individual.

It follows that a directive may not of itself impose obligations on an individual and that a provision of a directive may not be relied upon as such against such a person. However, where the conditions for direct effect are satisfied it is possible to bring a vertical action versus the state:

Case precedent – *Pubblico Ministero v Ratti*

Facts: Ratti had complied with the requirements of Directive 73/173 in packaging and labelling the solvent products his company produced. Italian law provided for different standards than the Directive and included penalties for non-compliance. The Italian authorities sought to prosecute Ratti under the domestic law. Ratti sought to protect himself by relying on the Directive. Italy had failed to implement Directive 73/173 by the time the deadline for implementation had passed.

The Court found in Ratti's favour concluding that:

> . . . a Member State which has not adopted the implementing measures required by the directive in the prescribed periods may not rely, as against individuals, on its own failure to perform the obligations the directive entails.

Principle: Direct effect can only be sought in relation to a directive after the date for implementation has passed.

Application: In answering problem questions, students should always check any information on dates provided carefully.

1. The content of the directive must satisfy the *Van Gend en Loos* test. It must contain rights which are sufficiently clear, precise and unconditional.
2. The action can only be brought after the implementation date has passed. What this means in practice is that any discretion a Member State has to implement a directive is removed once the deadline for implementation has passed. At that point the legal obligation on Member States to implement exists and they are legally required to give effect to the terms of the directive. At this point a Member State is prevented from relying on its own failure to implement as a defence to a claim bought by an individual on the basis of rights arising from the directive.
    Ratti also prepared another product, varnish, in accordance with the requirements of another directive, Directive 77/228, dealing with varnishes, but he failed in his attempt to rely on it in the face of prosecution by the Italian authorities. The implementation date had not yet passed for this Directive and, as the Court said, before the deadline for implementation has passed, 'the Member States remain free in that field'.
3. Only if the action is against the State – vertically, as in *Marshall* above. The court also introduced the notion of a wider state concept – the state emanation.

Summary: Conditions for the direct effect of directives

Condition	Key case	Principle	Practical application
Clear, precise, unconditional	*Van Gend en Loos*	The original criteria that need to be satisfied for direct effect	Check the wording of any law that might be provided in your question
The time for implementation	*Ratti*	The implementation date for the directive must have passed	Check any dates provided in the question to see if the member state has failed to meet the stated implementation deadline

Condition	Key case	Principle	Practical application
Vertical direct effect	*Marshall*	The action can only be brought against the state or a state emanation	Using case law, you may have to judge whether the body in the question is a state emanation

Students often confuse many of the terms in this area. You need to be able to clearly distinguish between direct effect and direct applicability and between vertical and horizontal direct effect. Remember that direct applicability does not produce guaranteed individual rights – merely that law exists. Direct effect allows for individuals to use rights in their national courts.

What is an emanation of the state?

The CJ in *Marshall* did not set out clear criteria for establishing when a body was an emanation of the state. It was evidently apparent from *Marshall* that a health authority would be considered an emanation of the state.

However, the CJ did provide more specific criteria in the following case.

Case precedent – *Foster v British Gas plc*

Facts: The action in *Foster* had been brought by six women who had been forced to retire the age of 60 in accordance with the policy of British Gas. This was five years earlier than their male counterparts were required to retire. The applicants sought to rely on Directive 76/207 (the Equal Treatment Directive). At the time of their dismissal, British Gas was a nationalised industry, although it had subsequently been privatised. The House of Lords sought a preliminary ruling from the CJ on whether, at the time of their dismissal, British Gas was a body of such a type that the applicants are entitled to rely directly upon Directive 76/207 in English courts and tribunals.

The CJ began by summarising the broad powers and duties that British Gas had under the Gas Act 1972 and the powers that the Secretary of State had over it under that Act. The court decided that British Gas was an emanation of the state.

Principle: That the definition of the state is a wide one.

Application: Students will have to apply the case law tests to decide on the question of whether a body is a state emanation.

How did the court in *Foster* reach its conclusion?

The CJ discussed two possible routes in deciding the case:

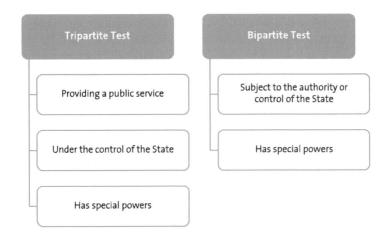

Tripartite Test	Bipartite Test
Providing a public service	Subject to the authority or control of the State
Under the control of the State	Has special powers
Has special powers	

The answer – The tripartite test

The CJ then provided its answer to the question asked by the House of Lords. In paragraph 22 and the operative part of the decision, it simply held that Directive 76/207 may be relied upon against a body which satisfied the tripartite test.

The answer left little doubt as to which test was to be applied to the facts of the case itself. But the overall judgment left uncertainty as to which test was supposed to be applied in other situations in order to identify an emanation of the state.

The UK approach

The House of Lords applied the CJ's ruling in *Foster* to the facts of that case in *Foster v British Gas (No. 2)* [1991] 2 AC 306. In accordance with the formal answer provided by the CJ, it applied the tripartite test and held that British Gas was an emanation of the State. Under the Gas Act 1972, British Gas provided a public service by supplying gas to citizens of the state generally. It did so under the control of the state as the Secretary of State could dictate its policies and the State retained its surplus revenue. British Gas also had a special monopoly power under which it could to prevent anyone else from supplying gas in the United Kingdom without its consent.

The tripartite test followed

Following this case, the tripartite test was also applied by the courts of England and Wales in the following two cases:

Doughty v Rolls-Royce Plc	Griffin v South West Water Services Ltd
Rolls-Royce was not an emanation of the state despite all of its shares being owned by the government and its nominees. It operated as a 'commercial undertaking' which traded with the government on an 'arm's-length' commercial basis. It was not providing a public service and it did not have any special powers.	A privatised water company satisfied all three elements of the tripartite test. It had been made responsible, pursuant to a measure adopted by the State, for providing a public service by acting as a water and sewage undertaker under statute. The Secretary of State had appointed it as the water and sewage undertaker for the South West and exercised wide-ranging powers of control over it. It also had a range of special powers such as to impose hosepipe bans, to make by-laws, to enter land and to lay pipes.

Nevertheless, this does not mean that the tripartite test was treated by the courts of England and Wales as the sole test. In *Doughty*, Lord Musthill opined that, whilst the tripartite test should be applied in a general case of the same type as *Foster*, the words 'included in any event' made it clear that the tripartite test was not to be applied in every case.

What is the current test for state emanation?

The first time that the CJ was called upon to revisit the question of what constitutes an emanation of the state was in the following case:

> ### Case precedent – *National Union of Teachers v Governing Body of St Mary's Church of England School (Aided) Junior School*

Facts: The Board of Governors of a Church of England School, which had voluntarily accepted state aid and entered the state education system, was held to be an emanation of the state.

Schiemann LJ held that it was wrong to treat the tripartite test in *Foster* as if it were a statutory definition. This case, he observed, was not of the same general type as *Foster* and *Doughty*. Those two cases involved commercial undertakings in which the government had a stake. This case involved the provision of a public service by a school which had entered the state school system. It was sufficient, he concluded, that the Board of Governors was providing a public service and that the Secretary of State and the Local Education Authority were able to exercise a sufficient degree of control over the school. There was no need to demonstrate any special powers.

Principle: The use of the bipartite test for state emanations.

Application: To demonstrate that in the UK the courts may use a different test for non-commercial bodies.

The CJ has applied both tests over the last 12 years.

Case precedent – *Kampelmann v Landschaftsverband Westfalen-Lippe*

Facts: This involved claims against a regional authority ('Landschaftsverband') responsible for, amongst other things, the construction, maintenance and management of highways; and against two public undertakings ('Stadtwerke'), each of which were responsible for the supply of energy to a town.

In reaching its decision, the CJ did not refer to the tripartite test at all. Instead, in accordance with the bipartite test from *Foster*, it held the Directive could be relied upon against organisations or bodies which are subject to the authority or control of the State *or* have special powers beyond those which result from the normal rules applicable to relations between individuals.

Principle: The bipartite test followed.

Application: There is no hard and fast approach to which test will be followed.

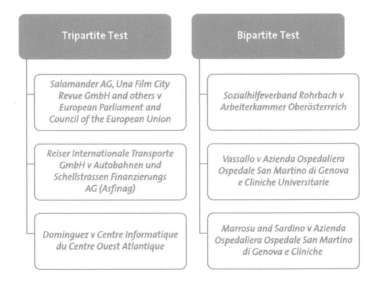

Tripartite Test	Bipartite Test
Salamander AG, Una Film City Revue GmbH and others v European Parliament and Council of the European Union	*Sozialhilfeverband Rohrbach v Arbeiterkammer Oberösterreich*
Reiser Internationale Transporte GmbH v Autobahnen und Schellstrassen Finanzierungs AG (Asfinag)	*Vassallo v Azienda Ospedaliera Ospedale San Martino di Genova e Cliniche Universitarie*
Dominguez v Centre Informatique du Centre Ouest Atlantique	*Marrosu and Sardino v Azienda Ospedaliera Ospedale San Martino di Genova e Cliniche*

Conclusion

It is perhaps helpful to remember that the CJ is able to transcend precedent in a way that is a lot harder for an English court and it may well simply be applying the approach most appropriate to the immediate factual circumstances of the case.

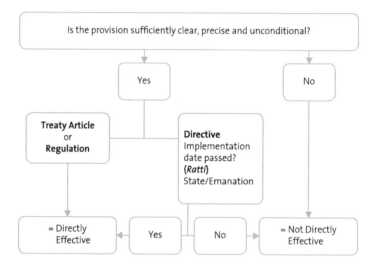

Putting it into practice

Directive 2011/56 (fictitious) has been introduced into the EU to ensure that the approach to online shopping is the same throughout the Member States.

Article 3 states:

> 'All member states must set up in their own states a fund of 50 million Euros in order to compensate consumers who have lost money as a result of a fraudulent online transaction.'

The deadline for implementation of the deadline was 1 June 2013. As yet, the UK has not implemented this directive.

On 15 June 2013, Marc ordered a laptop computer from an online retailer, Suez Plc, costing £550. After three weeks the computer had not arrived and, despite many attempts to contact the sellers, he has heard nothing. Marc is beginning to suspect that he has been the victim of a fraudulent website and is very worried about his financial loss.

However, he has read in the newspapers about a new EU law which he hopes will provide him with a solution.

Advise Marc.

Suggested solution

To start an action for direct effect, the first stage is to identify the form of EU law involved:

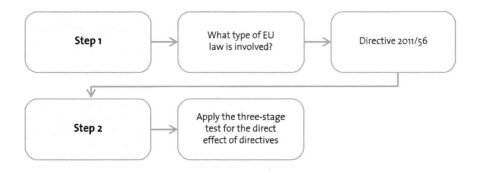

Once the type of law has been identified, the fact that it is a directive makes the application of the law more complicated than if the law was directly applicable (i.e. a Treaty article or a Regulation).

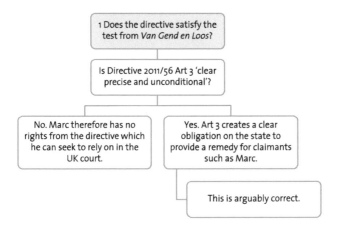

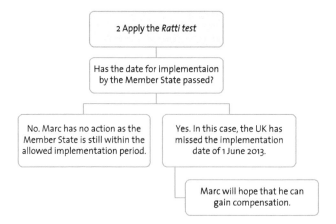

As Marc has satisfied the first two conditions he will be optimistic that he can succeed in a claim to recover his money. However, as a directive is not directly applicable and is for the Member State to implement, only a vertical direct effect action against the state will succeed.

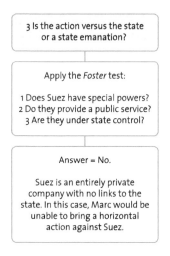

This situation illustrates the unfairness of the direct effect doctrine in that Marc is unable to get the compensation that the EU intended in the Directive. As such, he is a victim of the failure on the part of the UK to put the Directive into UK law within the required timeframe.

It was this perceived gap which led to the development of the doctrines of indirect effect and state liability as outlined in the next chapter.

Aim Higher

In the above problem, how would your answer differ if Marc had ordered his laptop from a website which sold ex-government equipment and divided the profits equally between the seller and the government source?

In such a scenario, you would need to discuss the application of the state emanation concept and associated cases. Arguably, a good case could be made for an element of state control in such a situation, therefore an action for direct effect could be attempted.

Table of key cases referred to in this chapter

Case name	Area of law	Principle
Alfons Lütticke GmbH v Hauptzollamt Saarlouis C57/65 [1966] ECR 205	Direct effect	This illustrates the principle that DE can be used to force MS to positively act.
Costa v ENEL C6/64 [1964] ECR 585	EU supremacy	The ECJ emphasised that MS sacrifice some of their sovereignty when joining the EU.
Defrenne v SABENA (No 2) C43/75 [1976] ECR 455	Horizontal direct effect	This was the first case to establish the principle of horizontal direct effect.
Doughty v Rolls-Royce Plc [1992] 1 CMLR 1045 CA	Emanations of the state	This was not such a body.
Dominguez v Centre Informatique du Centre Ouest Atlantique [2012] ECR 00	Emanations of the state	The tripartite test was applied.
Foster v British Gas plc C188/89 [1990] ECR I-3313	Emanations of the state	Three criteria were established to recognise such bodies.
Griffin v South West Water Services Ltd [1995] IRLR 15 HC	Emanations of the state	This was determined as an emanation.
Kampelmann v Landschaftsverband Westfalen-Lippe C243 to 258/96 [1997] ECR I-6907	Emanations of the state	The bipartite test was followed in this case.

Case name	Area of law	Principle
Marshall v Southampton and South West Area Health Authority (Teaching) (No 1) C152/84 [1986] ECR 723	Direct effect and Directives	This was the first case to establish the principle of vertical direct effect in relation to directives.
Marrosu and Sardino v Azienda Ospedaliera Ospedale San Martino di Genova e Cliniche Universitarie Convenzionate C53/04 [2006] ECR I-7213	Emanations of the state	The bipartite test was applied.
National Union of Teachers v Governing Body of St Mary's Church of England School (Aided) Junior School [1997] CMLR 630	Emanations of the state	The use of the bipartite test here to determine the school as an emanation.
Pubblico Ministero v Ratti C148/78 [1979] ECR 1629	Time limits for DE	Established that an action for DE cannot be brought until the date for implementation of a directive has expired.
Salamander AG, Una Film City Revue GmbH and others v European Parliament and Council of the European Union (T-172/98 and T-175/98 to T-177/98) [2000] ECR II-02487	Emanations of the state	The tripartite test was applied.
Sozialhilfeverband Rohrbach v Arbeiterkammer Oberösterreich C297/03 [2005] ECR I-4305	Emanations of the state	The bipartite test was applied.
Reiser Internationale Transporte GmbH v Autobahnen und Schellstrassen Finanzierungs AG (Asfinag) C157/02 [2004] ECR I-1477	Emanations of the state	The tripartite test was applied.
Van Gend en Loos C26/62 [1963] ECR1	Vertical direct effect	This was the first case to establish the principle of vertical direct effect.

Vassallo v Azienda Ospedaliera Ospedale San Martino di Genova e Cliniche Universitarie Convenzionate C180/04 [2006] ECR I-7251	Emanations of the state	The bipartite test was applied.

@ **Visit the book's companion website to test your knowledge**

❖ Resources include a subject map, revision tip podcasts, downloadable diagrams, MCQ quizzes for each chapter, and a flashcard glossary

❖ www.routledge.com/cw/optimizelawrevision

4

Indirect Effect and State Liability

Revision objectives

Understand the law
- Could you explain the concepts of indirect effect and state liability?

Remember the details
- Can you detail the tests for each?

Reflect critically on areas of debate
- Do you understand the underlying ideas behind both concepts?

Contextualise
- Can you see how these are an advance on the concept of direct effect?

Apply your skills and knowledge
- Can you apply this material in a problem style question?

Chapter Map 1 – indirect effect

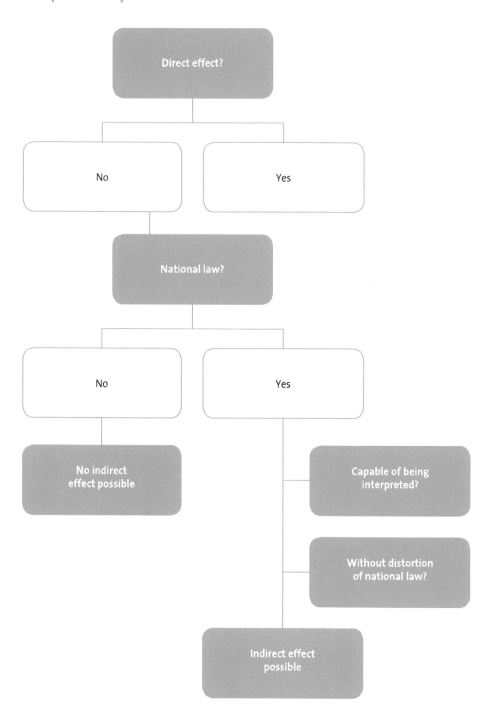

Introduction

The doctrine of direct effect only goes so far in providing a potential remedy for EU citizens. It was clear from the previous chapter that those citizens who wish to bring an action against a private body or who wish to rely on law which is not sufficiently clear enough may encounter obstacles in this regard.

This is especially the case with directives, which can only be used in actions versus emanations of the state. This potentially leaves the majority of EU citizens with little remedy in the event that their Member State either completely fails to implement a directive or implements in a way which fails to meet the purpose of the directive.

The Court of Justice met this need by developing two further routes for the individual to explore: indirect effect and state liability.

Indirect effect

In 1983, the CJ established that directives, even if not directly effective, are capable of having 'indirect effect' in that their provisions can be used by national courts in interpreting the meaning and scope of national legislation.

Case precedent – *Von Colson & Kamann v Land Nordhein-Westfalen*

Facts: Two female social workers applied for jobs with the prison service of a German Federal State but were rejected in favour of less well-qualified male applicants on the basis that problems may arise if deployed in a male prison. They argued that they had been discriminated against on the ground of sex.

A German law implementing Directive 76/207 (the Equal Treatment Directive) existed on which the women could rely. Their discrimination argument was successful but under national law they were only entitled to nominal damages in the form of travelling expenses. This appeared to fail to meet the obligation laid down in Art 6 of the ETD.

Principle: The CJ found that Article 6 of the ETD was not sufficiently clear, precise and unconditional to be directly effective, but turned to Article 5 EC (now see Article 4(3) TOTEU), which requires that Member States 'take all appropriate measures' to ensure that their obligations under EU law are fulfilled, and drew from this the principle of indirect effect.

Because Article 5 was binding on 'all authorities of Member States', the CJ found that national courts, as part of the state, are required to interpret domestic laws implementing a directive in conformity with the wording and purpose of the directive.

Application: The CJ left it to the West German court to apply the interpretative duty to its national law but made it clear that, whilst the Directive did not specify a form of sanction, any sanction that was imposed by the national court had to be such as to guarantee real and effective judicial protection of the right to equal treatment under the Directive and to have a real deterrent effect of the employer. Consequently, if an award of compensation was made, that award had to be adequate in relation to the damage sustained and therefore had to be more than purely nominal..

Indirect effect and horizontality

This case concerned a vertical claim by the two female social workers against an emanation of the state, the prison service of a German Federal State. However it is clear that the logic of the reasoning in *Von Colson* effectively dispenses with any requirement to distinguish between vertical and horizontal claims. An applicant can therefore bring an action using this doctrine against a public or private body. This principle was established in *Harz v Deutsche Tradax* (Case 79/83) [1984] ECR 1921.

The case had similar facts to *Von Colson* and had been referred to the CJ at the same time by the West German Labour Court. However, in contrast to *Von Colson*, the claim in Harz was made against a private company. That distinguishing fact was irrelevant in terms of the approach of the CJ which handed down its judgment on the same day as *Von Colson*.

Consequently, the interpretive duty imposed on national courts by the principle of indirect effect applies irrespective of whether a case can be characterised as vertical or horizontal and so applied as equally to the claimant in Harz as it had to the claimants in *Von Colson*.

Aim Higher

Consider how this new doctrine links to direct effect and attempts to solve the problems identified in that chapter. Then link this to the next section to see how IE and state liability are connected.

How was indirect effect received in the UK?

The UK courts have tended, at least initially, to be careful in their application of the *Von Colson* principle.

Case precedent – *Duke v G.E.C. Reliance Ltd*

Facts: Female employees had been forced to retire earlier than male employees. They sought to rely on Directive 76/207. GEC was not an emanation of the state and so the directive could not have direct effect in this case. The House of Lords had to determine whether the directive could be given indirect effect instead.

Principle: It held that the section 6(4) of the Sex Discrimination Act 1975, which specifically excluded involuntary retirement from the ambit of the Act, could not be interpreted in a way that gave indirect effect to the directive.

Application: Lord Templeman, who gave the lone judgment, stated that there was nothing in *Von Colson* which required the court to reach another conclusion by distorting the meaning of the Act.

This was a relatively narrow understanding of *Von Colson*.

Nevertheless, in accordance with that understanding, the House of Lords did prove willing to give indirect effect to national legislation in both *Pickstone* and *Litster* where the respective pieces of legislation in these two cases had each been made for the purpose of giving effect to a directive.

Case precedent – *Pickstone v Freemans plc*

Facts: The House of Lords was called upon to interpret the Equal Pay Act 1970, as amended by the Equal Pay (Amendment) Regulations 1983, in the light of the Directive 75/117 (the Equal Pay Directive).

These had been made to give effect to a judgment of the CJ which had held that the United Kingdom had failed to implement the Directive correctly.

The Regulations did so by adding a new section 1(2)(c) to the Act which provided that an 'equality clause' would be implied into an employment contract where a woman is employed on work of equal value to that of a man in the same employment.

Principle: The court resolved this by holding that, as the amendment was designed to comply with the directive, it would depart from the statute's normal unambiguous meaning to interpret it in conformity with the directive.

Application: This illustrates a narrowing of the indirect effect approach.

Case precedent – *Litster v Forth Dry Dock and Engineering Co Ltd*

Facts: This concerned Directive 77/187 which provided protection for the rights of employees in the event of a transfer of a business undertaking. The Transfer of Undertakings (Protection of Employment) Regulations 1981 were deliberately made to implement the directive in domestic law but were expressed to apply only to persons employed 'immediately before the transfer'.

On a strict interpretation of the UK Regulations the employees were not so employed as they had been dismissed an hour before the Forth Dry Dock business was transferred.

Principle: The HL construed the words 'immediately before' in the Regulations purposively and extended their application to cover those employees who would have been employed immediately before the transfer had they not been unfairly dismissed before the transfer.

The HL accepted that the Directive was designed to provide protection for employees from unfair dismissal by reason of a transfer of ownership and that the words of the Regulations should be interpreted in the light of this purpose.

Application: This judgment can be used to show how indirect effect is used to align domestic law with the law of the EU by a focus on the objective of the law rather than the words used.

In *Pickstone*, Lord Oliver justified the approach taken by the court in the following terms:

> . . . a construction which permits the section to operate as a proper fulfilment of the United Kingdom's obligation under the Treaty involves not so much doing violence to the language of the section as filling a gap by an implication which arises, not from the words used, but from the manifest purpose of the Act and the mischief it was intended to remedy.

Clarification and development of the *Von Colson* principle

The approach taken by the House of Lords in *Duke*, *Pickstone* and *Litster* was based on a UK understanding of what national courts were required to do under the *Von Colson* principle.

In a wider sense, this reflected ambiguities in the way that the CJ had outlined the nature and scope of the interpretative obligation in the case. In particular, two important questions remained to be resolved following the decision in *Von Colson*:

(1) To what extent could the principle of indirect effect apply to non-implementing laws and, in particular, those passed before the EU made a rule in the area covered by the existing national law?

(2) What was the scope of the qualification 'in so far as it is given discretion to do so under national law' referred to by the court in *Von Colson* in explaining how far national courts were required to go in interpreting national law in conformity with EU law?

Case precedent – *Marleasing SA v La Comercial Internacional de Alimentación SA*

Facts: A dispute between two private companies in Spain which concerned a conflict between an EU directive, the Company Law Directive 68/151 and a pre-existing Spanish law. Spain had not implemented the Directive and the deadline for implementation had passed.

Marleasing sought to have the contracts creating the defendant company declared null. Alleging the company had been created to defraud creditors, Marleasing argued 'lack of cause' as the ground for the declaration, a ground which came within the terms of the Spanish law.

In response, La Comercial relied on the later unimplemented directive, which included an exhaustive list of grounds on which a declaration of nullity could be declared. Lack of cause was not among them.

Principle: Direct effect was not available as a means through which Directive 68/151 could be given effect in the domestic law of Spain because the case involved a horizontal action between two private companies.

However, following *Von Colson*, indirect effect was available. The court held that the Spanish law had to be interpreted, as far as possible, in the light of the wording and the purpose of the directive to achieve the result pursued by the directive. However, what the court then did was to find that the conflict between the directive and the interpretation of the Spanish law allowing Marleasing's claim to proceed had to be resolved in favour of the directive.

The Spanish court was required to interpret the domestic law in conformity with the provisions of the directive.

Application: It is an approach which is difficult to reconcile with the 'as far as possible' qualification to the principle of indirect effect that the Court in *Marleasing* itself acknowledged.

The court's decision in *Marleasing* made clear that the provisions of an unimplemented directive could be used to interpret national law, even in a purely horizontal action between individuals.

It is also clear from this decision that it does not matter if the national law had been made before or after the directive: the directive can still be used to interpret that law.

Although the key conclusions of the court in *Marleasing* have mostly been accepted, there has been a pull back from the expansive interpretation approach adopted in the case.

Case precedent – *Wagner Miret v Fondo di Garantia Salarial*

Facts: Directive 80/987 required each Member State to establish a fund protecting employees from lost wages in the event of a company becoming insolvent. Spain had implemented the Directive, but it specifically excluded senior management from the ambit of the compensation fund it established.

As a senior manager of an insolvent company, and so a member of the excluded class, Miret could not apply to the fund for compensation. Instead, he sought to rely directly on Directive 80/987, which did not require or sanction the exclusion of senior management from compensation in the event of their company becoming insolvent.

Principle: The CJ held that the Directive was not directly effective because it was too imprecise to satisfy the conditions for direct effect. As to the operation of the principle of indirect effect, the Court again referred to the principle that national courts were required 'as far as possible' to interpret national law in conformity with the wording and purpose of a directive, but in this case the Court made clear that that was a matter for national courts to determine.

The CJ accepted that it appeared from the national court's reference that it was not possible to interpret the national law in a way that was consistent with the requirements of the Directive.

Application: A good illustration of the limits of the indirect effect doctrine where clear words make such an approach problematic.

Case precedent – *Evobus Austria GmbH v Niederösterreichischer*

Facts: Directive 92/13 required Member States to lay down appropriate procedures for reviewing the legality of the procurement process in specified sectors including transport. Austria had failed to do so. Evobus sought a review of a tendering procedure for the award of a public supply contract for buses.

Principle: The CJ first held that the right to review conferred by the Directive could not have direct effect as it did not specify which national bodies were to be the competent bodies for conducting a review and so it was not sufficiently clear and precise.

The court then considered indirect effect. It accepted that it was not possible to interpret Austrian law in a way that was consistent with the right to review under Directive as Austrian law specifically excluded authorities awarding transport sector contracts from its review system.

Application: Again, clear wording renders against the use of indirect effect.

Further limits
At this stage it is useful to highlight some other limits to the doctrine.

Implementation deadline for the Directive must have passed	Legal certainty and non-retroactivity
Adeneler v Ellinikos Organismos Galaktos (ELOG)	*Kolpinghuis Nijmengen BV*
The Grand Chamber of the CJ held that the obligation on national courts to interpret national law in conformity with a directive exists only once the deadline for the implementation of that directive has passed.	The Dutch authorities wanted to bring a criminal action against Kolpinghuis for marketing carbonated tap water as 'mineral water'. However, the Dutch law implementing Directive 80/777, which dealt with water purity, had not yet come into force. Consequently, they turned to an already existing Dutch regulation prohibiting marketing of water of 'unsound composition' and argued that the regulation should be interpreted so as to cover what Kolpinghuis had done in line with the provisions of the (unimplemented) Directive.
	A Member State cannot rely on a directive itself and independently of an implementing law to determine or aggravate criminal liability.

The UK post-*Marleasing*

Case precedent – *Webb v EMO Air Cargo (UK) Ltd (No 1)*

Facts: Webb had been employed on an indefinite contract to replace a person who was going on maternity leave. However, before she even started the job, she was dismissed, the reason being that she had also become pregnant.

The case involved application of the Sex Discrimination Act 1975 (the 'SDA') and possible conflict with the requirements of the Equal Treatment Directive 76/207.

Principle: National courts were required to construe domestic legislation in those areas covered by an EU directive 'so as to accord with the interpretation of the directive as laid down by the European Court'. This was so even where the legislation pre-dated the relevant directive, as did the SDA.

Application: Such an interpretation could only follow where it could be made 'without distorting the meaning of the domestic legislation'. Explaining what the 'as far as possible' requirement meant, he said, 'the domestic law must be open to an interpretation consistent with the directive whether or not it is also open to an interpretation inconsistent with it'.

In its judgment in *Webb v EMO Air Cargo (UK) Ltd (No. 2)*, made following this reference, the House of Lords concluded that it could interpret the SDA in conformity with the Equal Treatment Directive without distorting its meaning. Section 1(1)(a) of the SDA prohibited the discriminatory treatment of women on the ground of their sex. Section 5(3) stated discrimination was to be assessed on the basis of similar 'relevant circumstances' between the treatment of men and women at their workplace.

The CJ established that, by definition, only women can become pregnant and, consequently, dismissing them from work for the reason of pregnancy constituted direct discrimination as outlawed by the Directive.

In *Webb (No. 1)*, the House of Lords had interpreted 'relevant circumstances' under s 5(3) of the SDA as meaning simply not available for work and, as such, Webb's dismissal was not considered discriminatory, as both men and women could be dismissed for this reason.

Following the CJ's decision, the House of Lords focused on the fact that only women could become pregnant and now construed 'relevant circumstances' to mean unavailable for work by reason of pregnancy, which clearly could only affect a woman. Consequently, Webb's dismissal was found to be discriminatory.

Since *Webb*, British courts have attempted to interpret purposively any UK enactment consistently with the requirements of EU law, insofar as it is susceptible to such an interpretation.

More detailed guidance on what the interpretative obligation entails in England and Wales has been laid down by the Court of Appeal in *HM Revenue and Customs v IDT Card Services Ireland Ltd*.

The court outlined the following principles:

1 {
❖ There is no need to find that the statutory language should be ambiguous before interpreting the legislation.
}

2   ❖ The interpretation can change the meaning of the legislation in a way that involves a substantial departure from the language. It can read the language more restrictively or more expansively and can read words into the legislation.

3   ❖ However, the court must not rewrite legislation in a way that goes beyond interpretation. It cannot read words into the legislation that go against the grain of the legislation. Nor can it adopt a meaning that departs from a fundamental feature of the legislation or a cardinal principle of it.

4   ❖ The interpretation cannot entail the court making a decision which involves it making policy choices that it is not equipped to make or where there will be practical repercussions which the court is not equipped to evaluate.

Putting it into practice

Directive 2011/56 (fictitious) has been introduced into the EU to ensure that the approach to online shopping is the same throughout the Member States.

Article 3 states: 'All member states must set up in their own states a fund of 50 million Euros in order to compensate consumers who have lost money as a result of a fraudulent online transaction.'

The deadline for implementation of the deadline was 1 June 2013. As yet, the UK has not implemented this directive.

There is, however, a UK Consumer Act from 2009 (fictitious) which states the following: '... consumers who have suffered loss due to a fraudulent transaction may apply to the government for their lost to be reimbursed by the state ...'.

On 15 June 2013, Marc ordered a laptop computer from an online retailer, Suez Plc, costing £550. After three weeks had passed, the computer had not arrived and, despite many attempts to contact the sellers, he has been unsuccessful and has heard nothing. Marc is beginning to suspect that he has been the victim of a fraudulent website and is very worried about his financial loss.

However, he has read in the newspapers about a new EU law which he hopes will provide him with a solution.

Advise Marc.

Suggested solution

The key to the application of indirect effect is the understanding that this is essentially an interpretative approach requiring that national law is read in the light of EU law. This was introduced in *Von Colson* and subsequently developed through a sequence of cases.

Is there any national law?	
This can be an implementing directive as in *Von Colson*	Or it can be any pre-existing national law in a related area as in *Marleasing*. In this scenario, we have a piece of pre-existing UK legislation which appears to be in a similar legal area.

Is this law capable of being interpreted in the light of the EU law?	
Von Colson explained that this should be 'as far as possible'	However, there should be no distortion of the meaning of the domestic law as discussed in *Webb No 1*. In this case you would need to consider if the UK law could be read in the light of the EU law. It is arguable that this would be possible in order for the objective of the EU directive to be fulfilled.

Are there any other limits applicable?	
The interpretation should not go against the clear words as in *Evobus*.	The interpreatation should not go against legal certainty or create criminal liability as in *Kolpinghuis*. To interpret in this case would arguably not infringe these rules.

Conclusion

It is arguable that the UK courts would interpret the UK law in the light of the EU directive in order to achieve the aim of the objective. There would be some discussion over the discretionary word 'may' in the Act and the obligatory word 'must' in the directive but overall it is the case that such an interpretation would probably not distort the UK law.

State liability

This third approach sought to remedy the failings of both direct effect and indirect effect by seeking to place the burden squarely on the Member States.

The key case of *Francovich* created a three-stage test:

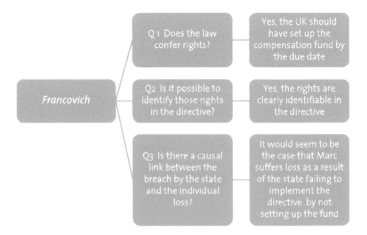

Conclusion

It is arguable that the failure of the UK to implement the directive and set up the compensation fund has caused Marc loss – he has a good claim for state liability versus the UK state using the *Frankovich* doctrine. In addition, in the case of *Dillenkofer* using the expanded doctrine, it was held that a failure by a MS to implement a directive would always be a sufficiently serious breach.

Aim Higher

In the above problem, how would your answer differ if the UK state had implemented the directive but had deliberately changed the terms in the Act to € 25 million and the UK had already awarded this amount resulting in an empty fund.

This could make it difficult to use indirect effect as the wording is clear and as such there could be a distortion of the law.

However, state liability would be possible using the expanded doctrine from *Brasserie de Pêcheur/Factortame* as this seems to be a sufficiently serious breach.

Table of key cases referred to in this section

Case name	Area of law	Principle
Adeneler v Ellinikos Organismos Galaktos (ELOG) C212/04 [2006] ECR I-6057	Implementation date and IE	There is no obligation to interpret by the national court until the implementation deadline has passed.

Case name	Area of law	Principle
Duke v G.E.C. Reliance Ltd [1988] 1 AC 618	Application of indirect effect	IE can be used as long as there is no distortion of the law in the interpretation adopted.
Evobus Austria GmbH v Niederösterreichischer Gebietskrankenkasse C111/97 [1998] ECR I-5411	Interpretation of the doctrine	As the Austrian legislation had clear exclusions, interpretation was not possible.
Harz v Deutsche Tradax C79/83 [1984] ECR 1921	Indirect effect and horizontal effect	The problem of horizontal DE and directives was solved.
HM Revenue and Customs v IDT Card Services Ireland Ltd [2006] EWCA Civ 29	The UK post-*Marleasing*	There are clear limits on the use of IE.
Kolpinghuis Nijmengen BV C80/86 [1987] ECR 3969	Legal certainty	The court cannot imply criminal liability where none is clearly stated in the national law.
Litster v Forth Dry Dock and Engineering Co Ltd [1990] 1 AC 546	Indirect effect in the UK	IE used to resolve a possible conflict with EU law.
Marleasing SA v La Comercial Internacional de Alimentación SA C106/89 [1990] ECR I-4135	Scope of indirect effect	The court clarified the meaning of 'as far as possible'.
Pickstone v Freemans plc [1989] AC 66	Indirect effect in the UK	IE used to resolve a possible conflict with EU law.
Von Colson and Kamann v Land Nordhein-Westfalen C14/83 [1984] ECR 18	Indirect effect	The creation of the doctrine.
Wagner Miret v Fondo di Garantía Salarial C334/92 [1993] ECR I-6911	Limiting of IE	The court pulled back and stated that interpretation is not possible if the MS law is clearly inconsistent with EU law.
Webb v EMO Air Cargo (UK) Ltd (No 2) [1995] 4 All ER 577	The UK post-*Marleasing*	The UK courts will only use IE if the law is susceptible to such use.

Chapter Map 2 – State Liability

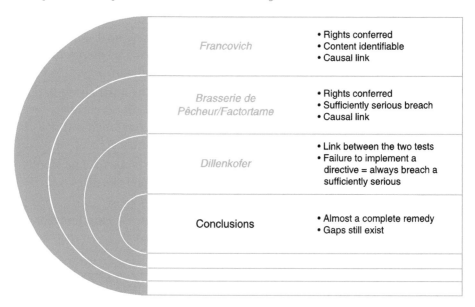

Francovich	• Rights conferred • Content identifiable • Causal link
Brasserie de Pêcheur/Factortame	• Rights conferred • Sufficiently serious breach • Causal link
Dillenkofer	• Link between the two tests • Failure to implement a directive = always breach a sufficiently serious
Conclusions	• Almost a complete remedy • Gaps still exist

Introduction

The principle of state liability allows an individual to recover compensation from a Member State where he or she has incurred loss as a result of the failure of that Member State to fulfil its obligations under EU law.

The CJ sought to lay responsibility for such failures fairly and squarely at the feet of Member States.

As such, the principle may provide a remedy to a person in circumstances where neither direct effect nor indirect effect is applicable. Equally, it also applies where both remedies are available.

Case precedent – *Francovich & Bonifaci v Italian Republic*

Facts: The employers of Francovich had gone bankrupt, resulting in Francovich not being paid outstanding wages. Directive 80/987 appeared to cover just such a situation. It required each Member State to establish guarantee institutions from which employees of insolvent companies could recover at least some of their lost wages. However, Italy had not implemented the Directive and the deadline for implementation had passed. As there was no national law under which Francovich and the other claimants could recover their losses, they turned to the Directive. The Italian court referred the case to the CJ.

Neither direct effect nor indirect effect could be relied upon in this case: the Directive's provisions did not satisfy the conditions for direct effect and there was no pre-existing national law which could be interpreted through indirect effect in conformity with its object and purpose.

Principle: What the CJ did find, however, was that Italy could be held liable for not having implemented this Directive in breach of its obligations under EU law:

> ... it is a principle of Community law that the Member States are obliged to make good loss and damage caused to individuals by breaches of Community law for which they can be held responsible.

Application: The CJ identified three conditions which had to be satisfied before the principle of state liability could take effect.

The *Francovich* conditions

1
- ❖ The first of those conditions is that the result prescribed by the directive should entail the grant of rights to individuals.

2
- ❖ The second condition is that it should be possible to identify the content of those rights on the basis of the provisions of the directive.

3
- ❖ The third condition is the existence of a causal link between the breach of the State's obligation and the loss and damage suffered by the injured parties.

The scope of the principle was clarified and the conditions for its application were refined in the joined cases of *Brasserie du Pêcheur SA v Germany* and *R v Secretary of State for Transport ex p Factortame Ltd (No. 4)* ('*Factortame III*').

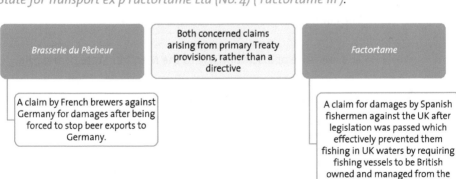

Brasserie du Pêcheur	Both concerned claims arising from primary Treaty provisions, rather than a directive	Factortame
A claim by French brewers against Germany for damages after being forced to stop beer exports to Germany.		A claim for damages by Spanish fishermen against the UK after legislation was passed which effectively prevented them fishing in UK waters by requiring fishing vessels to be British owned and managed from the United Kingdom.

The CJ confirmed the principle of state liability as set out in *Francovich*, but concluded that it was neither necessary that a breach be total in the sense that Italy's was in failing completely to implement a directive, but nor would any breach be enough to bring the principle into play. What was necessary was that the breach be 'sufficiently serious' (a requirement which replaces the second condition of the *Francovich* test where Member States have been left a degree of discretion under the relevant provision of EU law).

The revised conditions

1 ❖ The rule of law infringed must be intended to confer rights on individuals.

2 ❖ The breach must be sufficiently serious.

3 ❖ There must be a direct causal link between the breach of the obligation resting on the state and the damage sustained by the injured parties.

As to what constitutes a sufficiently serious breach, the court stated that the 'decisive' question was whether the Member State had 'manifestly and gravely disregarded the limits of its discretion'? The CJ further suggested a list of factors which could be taken into account in answering this question.

Common Pitfalls

You need to be clear on the difference between the three-stage test in *Francovich* and the three-stage test in *Brasserie du Pêcheur/Factortame*. Make sure you understand the reason for the expansion of the doctrine.

What is 'sufficiently serious'?

1 ❖ The clarity and precision of the rule breached.

2 ❖ The measure of discretion left to the Member State by the rule.

3 ❖ Whether the breach was intentional.

4 ❖ Whether the breach was excusable.

5 ❖ The extent to which a position taken by a Union institution may have contributed to the breach.

6 {
❖ The extent to which the Member States had adopted or retained national measures contrary to EU law.

The court also made clear that, beyond finding that a breach is sufficiently serious, there is no need to establish fault on the part of the Member State.

Nor is a breach restricted to failure to fully implement a directive: the principle may be applied with respect to any breach of EU law by a Member State, such as breach of the requirements of a Treaty article, as was at issue in *Brasserie du Pêcheur* (and *Factortame III*).

Sufficiently serious breach not proved	Sufficiently serious breach proved
R v HM Treasury, ex p British Telecommunications plc	*R v Ministry of Agriculture, Fisheries and Food, ex p Hedley Lomas (Ireland) Ltd*
While the court agreed that the UK had misunderstood what was required by the Directive and incorrectly transposed it into national law, it was held not to be liable in damages.	Hedley Lomas sought damages from the UK for refusing to grant export licences to allow live animals to be exported to Spain. The UK accepted that it had breached EU law dealing with the free movement of goods in not granting the licences, but it sought to justify that breach on grounds of animal welfare, a recognised ground for derogation under EU law in this area. In particular, the UK argued that Spanish slaughtering practice did not itself conform with therequirements of EU law.
The breach was excusable for a number of reasons, including: • the lack of precision in the relevant provision of the directive; • the UK's interpretation of what was required was made in good faith; • the same interpretation of the provision as made by the UK had also been made by other Member States; • that interpretation 'was not manifestly contrary to the wording of the directive or the objective pursued by it'; and • there was no guidance available through either case law of the CJ or from the Commission, which had not raised the matter with the UK when it had implemented the Directive.	in the absence of evidence supporting its case, the export ban could not be justified and the UK was found to be in breach. This 'mere infringement' of EU law was held by the Court to be sufficiently serious for the UK to be liable for the loss and damage Hedley Lomas suffered.
	The Court noted that: where . . . the Member State in question was not called upon to make any legislative choices and had only consider-ably reduced, or even no, discretion, the mere infringement of Community law may be sufficient to establish the existence of a sufficiently serious breach.

Case precedent – *Dillenkofer and others v Germany*

Facts: The CJ took the view that the conditions in *Francovich* and those in *Brasserie du Pêcheur* were the same in substance. It also made clear that failure by a Member State to implement a directive at all once the deadline for implementation has passed, as had occurred in *Francovich*, is of itself a sufficiently serious breach to establish state liability.

Principle: At first sight it appears that there are two tests for state liability – the *Francovich* test, which applies in situations of total breach where no discretion is left to a Member State, such as exists where a Member State fails to transpose a directive before the deadline for implementation has passed, and the *Brasserie du Pêcheur* test, which applies in circumstances where Member States have been left a degree of discretion under the relevant provision of EU law.

Application: *Dillenkofer* suggests that the *Brasserie du Pêcheur* test can in effect cover both situations, as failure to transpose a directive by the implementation deadline automatically constitutes a sufficiently serious breach. However, whether the CJ will ultimately reconcile the two tests in this way has not been decided.

State liability has been extended to include liability for damage caused to individuals by infringements of EU law coming from breaches of EU competition law by private individuals in *Courage Limited v Crehan*.

UK courts and state liability

The House of Lords applied the test mapped out by the CJ to the facts of the case in *R v Secretary of State for Transport, ex parte Factortame (No. 5)*. The case centred on Part II of the Merchant Shipping Act 1989 which had restricted the registration of fishing vessels to those which were British owned and managed in the United Kingdom. This had been drafted and proposed by the government and enacted into law by Parliament.

Lord Slynn held that the legislation did constitute a sufficiently serious breach. He accepted that the restrictions had been enacted in good faith with the intention of protecting British fishing communities and British fishing quotas rather than with the deliberate intention of harming Spanish fishermen and non-British citizens with stakes in British-registered fishing vessels. But the nationality condition was obviously discriminatory and in breach of the Treaty.

Officials and ministers were aware that there was a risk that, if enacted, the restrictions would be held to be in breach but the Government had considered it a risk worth taking. It had decided to press on with the introduction of the restrictions despite the firm and consistent warnings of the Commission that they would be contrary to the Treaty and the doubts of some of its own officials.

Conclusion

The CJ has attempted to integrate EU law into the national legal systems of Member States in ways which have given individuals a range of options through which to pursue rights under EU law in their national courts, culminating in the principle of state liability.

When will an applicant fail to have a remedy?

Direct effect may not be available because the conditions for direct effect are not satisfied or the claim is based on a directive and is between individuals.

Indirect effect may fail because it may not be 'possible' to interpret national law in conformity with the object and purpose of the relevant EU legislation.

State liability may not be established even where there is a breach because the breach may not be 'sufficiently serious'.

Key points for revision

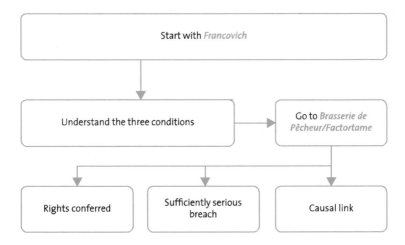

Start with *Francovich*

Understand the three conditions

Go to *Brasserie de Pêcheur/Factortame*

Rights conferred

Sufficiently serious breach

Causal link

Up for Debate

In your opinion, is it now the case that an individual in the EU will always have an available course of action when their state does not act in line with EU law?

Table of key cases referred to in this section

Case name	Area of law	Principle
Brasserie du Pêcheur SA v Germany *R v Secretary of State for Transport ex p Factortame Ltd (No 4)* (*'Factortame III'*) C46/93 & C-48/93 [1996] ECR I-1029 *R v Secretary of State for Transport, ex parte Factortame (No 5)* [2000] 1 AC 524	The extension of state liability	The ECJ extended the doctrine to all potential breaches of EU law, not just resulting from the failure to implement a directive.
Courage Limited v Crehan C453/99 [2001] ECR I-6297	Use of SL	Breaches of EU competition law by a MS.
Dillenkofer and others v Germany C178-9 & 188-190/94 [1996] ECR I-4845	The definition of 'sufficiently serious'	Failure to implement a directive is always regarded as a breach.
Francovich & Bonifaci v Italian Republic C6/90 & C9/90 [1991] ECR I-5357	The creation of state liability	The court decided that as the state was at fault which had led to damage being caused, the state should be held responsible for making good such loss.
R v HM Treasury, ex p British Telecommunications plc C392/3 [1996] ECR I-1631	The definition of 'sufficiently serious'	The court decided that the UK was not at fault citing various factors supporting the position of the UK government.
R v Ministry of Agriculture, Fisheries and Food, ex p Hedley Lomas (Ireland) Ltd C5/94 [1996] 2 CMLR 391	The definition of 'sufficiently serious'	The UK government was at fault for a deliberate breach of EU law.

@ Visit the book's companion website to test your knowledge

❖ Resources include a subject map, revision tip podcasts, downloadable diagrams, MCQ quizzes for each chapter, and a flashcard glossary

❖ www.routledge.com/cw/optimizelawrevision

5

Free Movement of Goods I: Articles 28–30 and 110 TFEU

Revision objectives

Understand the law
- Can you outline the concepts of custom duties, charges having equivalent effect and taxes?
- Which Articles are applicable here?

Remember the details
- Can you remember when charges and taxes fall outside the key law?
- Can you define each element of the key law?

Reflect critically on areas of debate
- Do you understand how a state may justify a charge or a tax?
- Can you define the concept of fiscal barriers accurately and critically discuss in relation to case law examples?

Contextualise
- Can you relate and compare these concepts to other areas of EU law such as the non-fiscal barriers to trade?

Apply your skills and knowledge
- Could you complete an essay or problem question in this area?

Chapter Map

Fiscal Barriers
Article 30 or Article 110

Charge | Tax

Article 30

- **Customs Duty**
  - Levy on imports (e.g. *Van Gend En Loos*)
- **Charge having equivalent effect**
  - Any pecuniary charge imposed by reason of the fact that the goods cross a frontier (*Commission v Italy (Statistical Data)*)

Charges outside Article 30

- *Commission v Germany*:
- A Tax (*Bresciani* and *Dansk Denkavit*)
- Charge for a service to the importer (*Commission v Belgium (Warehouses)*)
- Charge for inspections carried out to fulfil obligations imposed by EU law (*Commission v Germany*)
- *Commission v Netherlands*:
- Charge for obligatory inspections imposed on all member states by an international treaty

Article 110 (1) – Similar products

- **Are the goods similar?**
- Test = similar characteristics and same needs (*Commission v Denmark*)

Article 110 (1) – Similar products

- **If so, are the imported goods discriminated against?**
  - Direct discrimination? (e.g. *Commission v Italy (Regenerated Oil)*)
  - Indirect discrimination? OK if:
    - Based on objective criteria; and
    - Pursues economic policy objectives which are compatible with EU law; and
    - The detailed rules avoid any form of discrimination (*Chemical Farmaceutici*)

No | Yes

Article 110(2) – Non similar goods

- **Are the goods in competition,**
- even partial, indirect or potential, with products of the importing country? (*Commission v France (Spirits)*)
- If so, does the tax have **protective effect?**

Introduction

One of the fundamental aims of the EU is to ensure free movement throughout the Union – this extends to goods, services, people and capital and is stated as follows:

Article 26(2) TFEU

'The internal market shall comprise an area without internal frontiers in which the free movement of goods, persons, services and capital is ensured in accordance with the provisions of the Treaties.'

In the course of this book, we will address these key issues starting in this chapter with free movement of goods and in particular, the law relating to fiscal barriers to trade.

The key Treaty articles

On entering the state	Within the state
• Article 30	• Article 110
• Customs duties	• Tax on similar goods
• Charges having equivalent effect	• Tax on non-similar goods

These prohibitions – Articles 30 and 110 – concern barriers to trade between Member States that are of a *fiscal* nature. The broad difference between Articles 30 and 110 is that the former prohibits charges that are levied simply because goods have crossed the frontier of the state, whereas the latter regulates charges that are levied as a system of internal taxation within the state.

Part 1: Article 30: TFEU customs duties and charges having equivalent effect

---

Article 30

'Customs duties on imports and exports and charges having equivalent effect shall be prohibited between Member States. This prohibition shall also apply to customs duties of a fiscal nature.'

Article 30 thus prohibits two types of charge imposed as a result of crossing the border.

Customs duties

These are charges which, broadly, are imposed at the border usually by customs on the importer or exporter. Article 30 prohibits such between Member States. It does not matter how small the charge is as any barrier to trade is regarded as detrimental to the wider notion of a customs union.

Such charges make the imported good more expensive to the consumer thus placing them at a disadvantage in the domestic market providing an unfair advantage to the domestic national product.

Case precedent – *NV Algemene Transport en Expeditie Onderneming van Gend en Loos v Nederlandse Administratie der Belastingen* (the '*Van Gend en Loos*' decision)

Facts: Van Gend en Loos imported urea formaldehyde from West Germany in 1960 and was charged a customs duty by the Dutch authorities.

Principle: Van Gend en Loos, was entitled to invoke Article 30 to argue that a customs duty imposed on this product was not permissible. The case also established that Article 30 was capable of having direct effect.

Application: The wider point is that charges by virtue of crossing the border will fall within Article 30 and can never be justified by the state.

What matters is not the purpose of the charge but its effect.

Case precedent – *Commission v Italy* (the '*Italian Art*' case)

Facts: An Italian tax on the export of artistic heritage solely aimed at its retention and not to raise revenue was challenged as being in breach of Article 30.

Principle: The charge was held to be illegal as imposing a duty on the export of goods cannot be justified no matter what the reason. The CJ held that goods are products that 'can be valued in money and which are capable, as such, of forming the subject of commercial transactions'.

Application: This shows that even if the state can prove a convincing argument for the charge, it will fail: 'bare' customs duties can never be justified under Article 30.

Charges having equivalent effect

Article 30 also prevents states from imposing charges which are disguised customs duties. These are called charges having equivalent effect (CEEs).

The CJ has illuminated the nature of CEEs in a number of decisions.

Case precedent – *Commission v Italy* (the *'Statistical Levy'* case)

Facts: Italy imposed a levy on all imports and exports for the purpose of collecting statistical material relating to its trade patterns that, the Italian government argued, was of benefit to traders.

Principle: The CJ regarded the levy as a CEE that was prohibited by Article 30. It defined a CEE thus:

> Any pecuniary charge, however small and whatever its designation and mode of application, which is imposed unilaterally on domestic or foreign goods by reason of the fact that they cross a frontier and which is not a customs duty in the strict sense constitutes a charge having equivalent effect . . . even if it is not imposed for the benefit of the State, is not discriminatory or protective in effect and if the product on which the charge is imposed is not in competition with any domestic product.

In this case the statistics compiled and offered were of no use to the importer so the charge failed under Article 30.

Application: The case did offer the possibility of a defence for Member States. If a genuine benefit had been derived this might have been allowed by the CJ.

Common Pitfalls

Students are not always clear on the distinctions between customs duties and charges having equivalent effect. Remember, in the former, any charge stands on it's own and is not coupled with a service or other act by the offending state.

Following on from the definition of a CEE, the CJ elaborated on the meaning of non-protectionist in the following case.

Case precedent – *Sociaal Fonds voor de Diamantarbeiders v Chougol Diamond Co*

Facts: A charge on diamonds imported into Belgium was regarded as a CEE even though it was clearly not protectionist in nature – Belgium did not produce diamonds. The purpose of the charge was to fund additional social security benefits for Belgian diamond workers.

Principle: The CJ confirmed that customs duties and CEEs were prohibited regardless of the purpose for which they were introduced.

Application: The important point is that the effect of the charge was that the imported diamonds became less competitive.

Charges outside the scope of Article 30

However, there are a number of charges which the CJ have designated as falling outside the scope of Article 30. These exceptions were established in the case of *Commission v Germany* (Case 18/87) [1988] ECR 5427:

- ❖ if the charge 'relates to a general system of internal dues applied systematically and in accordance with the same criteria to domestic and imported products' alike; or
- ❖ if the charge constitutes payment 'for a service in fact rendered to the economic operator of a sum in proportion to the service'; or
- ❖ if the charge 'attaches to inspections carried out to fulfil obligations imposed by Community law'.

We will now consider each of these exceptions.

Internal tax

If the situation in point 1 above is established, the charge will fall to be evaluated under Article 10 rather than Article 30 because it will be in the nature of an internal tax rather than a charge that depends on the product crossing a frontier.

There are two contrasting cases to consider:

Dansk Denkavit ApS v Danish Ministry of Agriculture	*Bresciani v Amministrazione Italiana delle Finanze*
❖ The CJ held that a charge levied to fund the cost of checking imported samples of foodstuffs for quality, which was imposed using the same criteria as applied to domestic products, was not a CEE but part of an internal system of dues covered by Article 110. ❖ No breach by Denmark.	❖ The public health inspections on domestic and imported cowhides were seen by the CJ as being in the public interest and so should be paid for out of public funds (i.e. taxation). However, because there were different criteria for the levies on domestic goods and imports, the CJ decided that it could not be assessed as internal dues. ❖ Breach by Italy.

Therefore, to be seen as an internal tax, the charge must be systematically applied using the same criteria on domestic and imported goods alike.

Payment for services rendered

The CJ has ruled that a charge that is proportionate consideration for a genuine service that is of direct benefit to the importer or exporter will not be classified as a CEE. However, it is rare for this to succeed as demonstrated by cases of the *Statistical Levy* case and *Bresciani* where the charges imposed by the Italian state both fell within Article 30.

The key case is:

Case precedent – *Commission v Belgium* (the '*Customs Warehouses*' case)

Facts: Where the Belgian government charged for the use of a special warehouse within the country where customs clearance could be completed. The CJ held that the charge was a CEE – where payment of storage charges is demanded in relation to imported products solely in connection with the completion of customs formalities, it could not be regarded as consideration for a service actually rendered to the importer.

Principle: In this case, the CJ laid down that the charge in question will not be seen as a CEE where the following conditions are satisfied:

❖ it is consideration for a service rendered;
❖ it is of benefit to the importer; and
❖ the amount charged is commensurate with the costs of the service provided.

Application: The state can argue a benefit only if it falls within the criteria above.

Inspections required by EU law

Common Pitfalls

You need to understand the difference between the application of Articles 30 and 110.

As a rough guide, the former is usually enforced at the border, the latter often found in relation to an internal sales tax.

If a charge is imposed by the state because *they have due to the EU* then this falls outside Article 30.

Case precedent – *Commission v Germany*

Facts: The German Government charged a fee to cover the costs of veterinary inspections on imported live animals. The inspections were required under a Directive regulating the protection of animals during international transport. The CJ held that the inspection fee was not a CEE.

Principle: The court set out four requirements that need to be fulfilled in order for an inspection charge not to constitute a CEE:

❖ the charge must not exceed the actual costs of the inspections;
❖ the inspections must be obligatory and uniform for all the relevant products in the Union;
❖ the inspections must be prescribed by EU law in the general interest of the Union; and
❖ the inspections must promote the free movement of goods, in particular by neutralising obstacles that could have arisen from unilateral inspection measures.

Application: This also applies if the inspection has been imposed as a result of an international convention as established in *Commission v Netherlands*.

Part 2: Article 110 TFEU: Discriminatory internal taxation

Article 110

'(1) No Member State shall impose, directly or indirectly, on the products of other Member States any internal taxation of any kind in excess of that imposed directly or indirectly on similar domestic products.
(2) Furthermore, no Member State shall impose on the products of other Member States any internal taxation of such a nature as to afford indirect protection to other products.'

Case precedent – *Commission v France (Reprographic Machinery)* (Case 90/79) [1981] ECR 283

Facts: France had imposed a levy on reprographic machinery such as offset printing machines, microfiche scanners and photocopiers. Only 1% of the reprographic equipment put into the French market was produced in France. The remaining 99% was imported. The Commission argued that this meant that, in practice, the levy was borne by importers alone and so constituted a CEE.

Principle: The CJ held that the fact that French production was extremely limited compared to imports did not in itself justify the conclusion drawn by the Commission. The levy was part of a general system of internal dues because of the reason for which the levy was imposed, the purpose for which the money was to be used and the fact that it formed part of a wider tax scheme:

> 'a general system of internal dues applied systematically and in accordance with the same criteria to domestic products and imported products alike.'

Application: This illustrates that a genuine tax is not excluded by Article 110.

Whereas Article 30 broadly outlaws charges by virtue of crossing the border, Article 110 is designed to ensure that internal fiscal barriers to trade, such as discriminatory taxes are eliminated. This article is also directly effective *(Lütticke (Alfons) GmbH v Hauptzollamt Saarlouis)*. However, Article 110 does not cover taxes imposed by the state which are non-discriminatory.

Article 110 works as follows:

Article 110(1) similar goods	Article 110(2) Non-similar goods
Prohibits discriminatory taxation in regard to the imported goods and similar domestic goods.	Prohibits Member States from using taxation to protect domestic goods that, though not similar to the imported goods, are in competition with them.

Article 110(1) – similar products
It is unlawful under Article 110(1) for Member States to tax similar imported and domestic goods at different levels. Two questions need to be asked: first, are the goods in question similar and, second, does the taxation regime of the Member State discriminate against the imported goods either directly or indirectly?

How does the court decide which goods are similar?
This is not a question of identical goods but instead one that judges similarity on their similar and comparable use *(Commission v France* (the '*Spirits*' case).

The central test as established in *Rewe-Zentrale des Lebensmittel-Großhandels GmbH v Hauptzollamt Landau/Pfalz* is whether, at the same stage of production or marketing, the products had similar characteristics and met the same needs from the point of view of consumers.

The following cases offer an interesting contrast.

	Similar	Non-similar
Case Name	*Commission v Denmark*	*John Walker & Sons Ltd v Ministeriet for Skatter og Afgifter*
Facts	Wine made from grapes was taxed at a lower rate than wine made from fruit. All wine made from grapes was exclusively imported into Denmark. In contrast, liqueur type fruit wine was almost exclusively produced in Denmark whilst table wine made from fruit was typically produced in Denmark.	A higher rate of tax was imposed by Denmark on whisky (of foreign manufacture) than imposed on fruit liqueur wine (of domestic manufacture).
CJ decision	The CJ held that wine made from fruit and wines made from grapes were similar.	The CJ held that they are not similar as their characteristics are manifestly different.
Rationale	They had similar manufacturing processes and met the needs of the consumer as they can be consumed in the same way: used to quench thirst, as refreshments and at meal times. The alcohol content was also broadly the same.	Fruit liqueur wine is a fruit-based product obtained by natural fermentation. Scotch whisky is a cereal-based product obtained by distillation. The alcoholic strength of Scotch whisky is 40% by volume whereas the alcoholic strength of liqueur fruit wine does not exceed 20% by volume.

A specific illustration of the way that the CJ has applied its guidance on similarity in relation to cars can be seen in *Tarantik v Direction des Services Fiscaux de Seine et Marne*.

Here it was held that:

> Products such as cars are similar for the purposes of the first paragraph of Article 95 of the Treaty [now Article 110 TFEU] if their characteristics and the needs which they serve place them in a competitive relationship ... in relation to cars, the degree of competition between two models depends on the extent to which they meet various requirements regarding price, size, comfort, performance, fuel consumption, durability, reliability and other matters.

Once similar goods are involved, the next enquiry is whether the Member State has discriminated against the imported goods. This may be direct or indirect, and different approaches are adopted by the CJ depending on the type of discrimination.

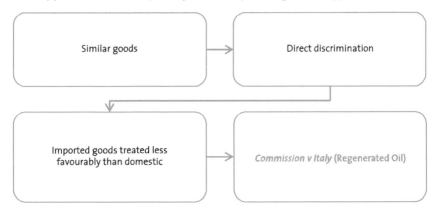

The Italian government had an ecological policy of charging lower tax on the sale of regenerated oil than that imposed on normal oil.

This benefit was only available to domestic oil producers. Italy argued that it had no way of knowing whether imported oil was regenerated or not.

The CJ held that this could not justify the direct discrimination against foreign regenerated oil and was hence a breach of Article 110(1).

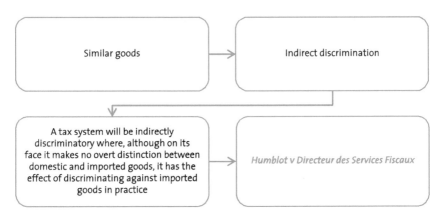

The tax regime involved a tiered system comprising two distinct taxes on cars. A differential tax imposing a gradually increasing rate of tax to a maximum of 1,100frs was applied on all cars up to an engine size of 16 CV. Any car with an engine over 16 CV was subject to a special tax at a high flat rate of 5,000frs. This was evidently almost five times the level of tax applicable to cars of 16 CV. On its face, this system did not treat imported cars less favourably than domestic cars. However, France did not produce any cars with an engine size above 16 CV.

The CJ held that, whilst Member States were free to subject cars to a road tax which increased progressively on the basis of objective criteria, this tax system manifestly exhibited both discriminatory or protective features contrary to Article 110 as, in practice, only imported cars were subject to the special tax whilst all domestic cars were liable to the distinctly more advantageous differential tax.

However, it may be the case that a tax may be justifiable even though it appears discriminatory on the surface.

Case precedent – *Commission v Greece*

Facts: This case involved the taxation of cars. Greece had imposed two taxes which increased on the basis of the cylinder capacity of the car. The increase in the taxes became more pronounced at 1,201cc and again at 1,801cc. Indeed, one of the taxes, which was payable when the car was first registered, rose by 50% between 1,800cc and 1,801cc. Greece justified this on the basis of social policy. However, it only produced cars up to 1,600cc.

Principle: The CJ emphasised that setting levels of taxation on the basis of social policy was not, in itself, incompatible with Article 110 and held that the Commission had failed to prove that the tax system actually had a discriminatory or protective effect against imported cars. Any consumers who were discouraged from buying a car over 1,800cc would be able to choose from the range of cars between 1,800cc and 1,600cc, which were still all imported in any event, or from the range of cars below 1,600cc which comprised both imported models and models manufactured in Greece.

Application: It should be noted that in this case the disparity in the levels of taxation was not as extreme as they were in *Humblot* demonstrating when a tax will be acceptable.

Article 110(2) TFEU: Non-similar products

Article 110(2) regulates the taxation of products which are not similar. It prohibits the imposition of any taxation on products imported from other Member States which is of such a nature as to afford indirect protection to domestic products.

The court in the following case held that Article 110(2) applied to goods that 'without being similar within the meaning of the first paragraph, are nonetheless in competition, even partial, indirect or potential, with certain products of the importing country'.

Case precedent – *Commission v France* (the '*Spirits*' case)

Facts: France had imposed an additional manufacturing tax on spirits obtained from cereals (such as whisky and Geneva) which was not imposed on spirits made from fruit and wine (such as brandy and Calvados). Nearly all cereal-based spirits were imported.

Principle: The CJ concluded that there was no need to determine whether they were similar products as it was impossible reasonably to contest that cereal-based spirits were in at least partial or potential competition with domestically produced wine and fruit-based spirits; it was also impossible to deny that the tax had protective effect. The two types of spirits had sufficient characteristics in common to constitute, at least in certain circumstances, an alternative choice for consumers.

Application: The approach of the court reflected an economic analysis based on the substitutability of the products: if one product is rendered more expensive, are consumers likely to switch to the other product?

The following cases offer an interesting contrast.

	In competition	Not in competition
Case Name	*Commission v UK* (the '*Wine and Beer*' case)	*Commission v Belgium*
Facts	The Commission had brought infringement proceedings against the United Kingdom for imposing a higher rate of tax on wine than on beer. It contended that beer and wine were in competition and that, since the United Kingdom had joined the European Communities, there had been a relative increase in duty on wine of 102% compared to a relative increase for beer had been 59% so that the tax burden on wine judged by volume had become approximately five times that of beer. This had the effect of branding wine as a luxury product.	Wine in Belgium was subject to a VAT rate of 25% whilst beer was subject to a rate of 19%.

	In competition	Not in competition
CJ decision	The CJ concluded that, in view of the substantial differences in the quality and price of wine, the decisive competitive relationship was between beer and the lightest and cheapest varieties of wine. It found that, irrespective of whether the tax ratio between these two kinds of beverages was judged by reference to volume or to alcohol content or by comparing tax as a proportion of the average price, it was clear that the tax burden on the cheaper types of wine was considerably higher than that on beer.	The CJ reiterated that wine and beer were in a competitive relationship and held that, in determining the protective effect of the tax system, the essential question is therefore whether or not the tax is of such a kind as to have the effect, on the market in question, of reducing potential consumption of imported products to the advantage of competing domestic products.
Rationale	This did have the effect of stamping wine with the hallmarks of a luxury product which could scarcely constitute a genuine alternative to beer in the eyes of the consumer.	The CJ concluded that, as the retail price of a litre of wine in Belgium was four times that of beer, the Commission had *failed to prove* that the difference of only 6% between the VAT rates applied to the two products was capable of influencing consumer behaviour and therefore of having a protective effect in favour of beer.

Cases where there is no similar or competing product

Where a Member State does not, itself, produce any similar product to the product being imported, Article 110 is, nevertheless, potentially of application. Article 110, rather than Article 30, will apply provided the tax fits within the general scheme of taxation applied systematically to categories of products in accordance with objective criteria, without reference to the origin of the product.

Aim Higher

In your opinion, do you think the approach in this area is heavy handed and that the MS should have greater freedom when it comes to their own tax regimes? If MS have flexibility in this area, what might this do to harmonisation of the law and the single market concept?

Case precedent – *Cooperativa Co-Frutta Srl v Ammistrazione delle Finanze dello Stato*

Facts: This concerned Italy's imports of bananas, a fruit produced by Italy only in negligible amounts. An importer challenged the tax that Italy imposed on bananas, arguing that no equivalent tax was charged in respect of other fruit which was grown in Italy. While the CJ accepted that bananas and table fruit had different characteristics (and hence the Italian government had not breached Article 110(1)) they could still be in partial competition with each other, so breaching Article 110(2).

Principle: The court held that Article 110 rather than Article 30 applied, because the tax was part of a general system of dues applied systematically to a category of product in accordance with objective criteria. On analysis, the tax violated Article 110(2) because the tax had a protective effect; the tax was equivalent to half the import price of bananas, while no tax applied to competing, non-similar table fruit products.

Application: The decision that such a levy is a tax and not a CEE is common sense. The alternative decision would mean that no Member State would be able to place a levy on any item it did not produce itself.

Remedies under Article 110(1) and 110(2)

It is important to have regard to the different remedies that follow where the Commission brings successful proceedings under Article 110(1) as compared with Article 110(2). Where the court finds that Article 110(1) has been infringed, the Member State must equalise the tax regime in respect of the similar product (for example, by applying the same tax rate to fruit wine and wine made from grapes). Where Article 110(2) has been violated, the remedy required of the Member State is different. The protective effect needs to be removed, which may not necessarily require equalisation between the non-similar products. For example, after the *Wine and Beer* case, the UK Government lowered the tax on wine and increased the tax on beer, but did not apply the same regime to both.

Putting it into practice

Pierrot SA is a French company which makes toys for children. Having consolidated themselves in the French market they are looking to expand into other EU states. However, they have been advised by their lawyers of the following:

1   In the UK, imported toys are subject to an inspection fee of £2.00 per item upon entry.

2   In Spain, all toys are inspected before sale and an annual fee of €300 is levied
     on firms selling toys in Spain.
3   In Germany, military and war toys are subject to a sales tax of 20%. Few
     German companies make such toys and the majority are imports.

Advise Pierrot if they can challenge any of the above charges.

Suggested solution

The UK

One of the key skills is to identify the type of charge and apply the applicable rule. A
good 'rule of thumb' approach is that charges at the border will usually fall within
Article 30 whilst those internally will engage Article 110.

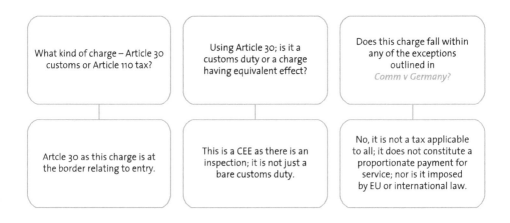

Conclusion

Pierrot could successfully challenge the charge using Article 30 and the case of
Bresciani seems appropriate to apply.

Spain

A key indicator of whether a charge is in breach of Article 30 is if the charge is
applicable to all manufacturers or is only aimed at importers.

This is clearly a fiscal charge placed on toy manufacturers but in this case
it is applicable to all irrespective of origin. This scenario reflects the crossover
between Articles 30 and 110 which act in tandem to prevent abuses by Member
States.

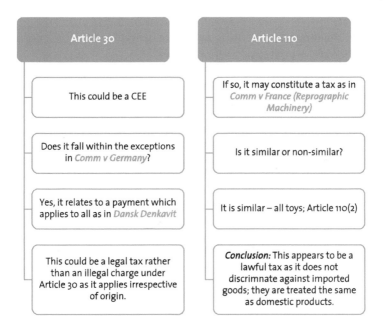

Germany

A key issue for the courts is whether the charge makes it more difficult for the importer. This can be more difficult to identify than a directly discriminatory charge or tax.

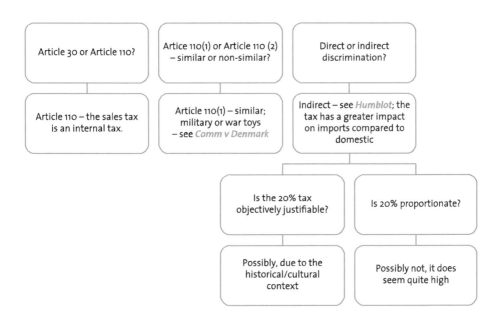

Conclusion

Pierrot could challenge the tax using Article 110(1) and *Humblot* as it does seem to be a disproportionate, arguably protectionist, tax.

Aim Higher

How would your answer differ if Germany made absolutely no toys of this kind? This would involve a discussion of non-similar goods under Article 110(2) and the *Co-Frutta* case.

Table of key cases referred to in this chapter

Case name	Area of law	Principle
Bresciani v Amministrazione Italiana delle Finanze C87/75 [1976] ECR 129	Internal tax	A charge imposed on cow hide importers was deemed to be an illegal tax.
Commission v Belgium C256/85 [1987] ECR 3299	Article 110 – Non-similar	The higher VAT rates on beer compared to wine were deemed not to be protective.
Commission v Belgium (the '*Customs Warehouses*' case) C132/82 [1983] ECR 1649	Payment for services rendered	A charge for storing goods in a warehouse was deemed to be in breach of Article 30.
Commission v Denmark C106/84 [1986] ECR 833	Article 110 – Similar goods	Drinks made from grapes and fruit were deemed to be similar.
Commission v France (*Reprographic Machinery*) C90/79 [1981] ECR 283	Tax under Article 110	This provides a clear definition of a tax falling outside Article 110.
Commission v France (the '*Spirits*' case) C 168/78 [1980] ECR 347	Article 110 – Similar Goods	Similarity is judged on similar and comparable use.
Commission v Germany C18/87 [1988] ECR 5427	Exceptions to Article 30	Three key exceptions were established in this case.
Commission v Greece C132/88 [1990] ECR I-1567	Indirect discrimination	Higher taxes on larger engine sizes were acceptable as they could be justified and rose incrementally.

Commission v Italy (the *'Italian Art'* case) C7/68 [1968] ECR 423	Customs duties	A good reason for a duty will still fail under Article 30.
Commission v Italy (*Regenerated Oil*) C21/79 [1980] ECR	Direct discrimination	As the importers could not benefit from the lower tax rates enjoyed by domestic producers, Article 110 was breached.
Commission v Italy (the *'Statistical Levy'* case) C24/68 [1969] ECR 193	Charges having equivalent effect	A charge for information provided to importers into Italy was deemed to be a breach.
Commission v Netherlands C89/76 [1977] ECR 1355	International inspections	These fall outside the scope of Article 30.
Commission v UK (the *'Wine and Beer'* case) C170/78 [1980] ECR 417 and [1983] ECR 2265	Article 110 – Non-similar	The higher tax on beer was of a level deemed to be disproportionate and protectionist.
Cooperativa Co-Frutta Srl v Ammistrazione delle Finanze dello Stato C193/85 [1987] ECR 2085	Article 110 – Non-similar	Although Italy has a small banana-growing industry, they could still discriminate against importers.
Dansk Denkavit ApS v Danish Ministry of Agriculture C29/87 [1988] ECR 2965	Internal tax	An inspection charge on all manufacturers was a legal tax.
Humblot v Directeur des Services Fiscaux C112/84 [1985] ECR 1367	Indirect discrimination	The large increase in tax overdue to larger engine size was judged as disproportionate and in breach.
John Walker & Sons Ltd v Ministeriet for Skatter og Afgifter C243/84 [1986] ECR 875	Article 110 – Similar goods	Drinks made from grapes and grain were deemed to be non-similar.
Lütticke (Alfons) GmbH v Hauptzollamt Saarlouis C57/65 [1966] ECR 205	Article 110	This established the article as directly effective.

Case name	Area of law	Principle
NV Algemene Transport en Expeditie Onderneming van Gend en Loos v Nederlandse Administratie der Belastingen (the '*Van Gend en Loos*' decision) C26/62 [1963] ECR 1	Customs duties	The Dutch breached EU law in imposing a customs duty by virtue of goods crossing the border.
Rewe-Zentrale des Lebensmittel-Großhandels GmbH v Hauptzollamt Landau/ Pfalz C45/75 [1976] ECR 181	Article 110 – Similar goods	Do the products have similar characteristics and met the same needs from the point of view of consumers?
Sociaal Fonds voor de Diamantarbeiders v Chougol Diamond Co C2 & 3/69 [1969] ECR 211	Charges having equivalent effect	A good reason for a duty will still fall under Article 30 – in this case, support for diamond workers.
Tarantik v Direction des Services Fiscaux de Seine et Marne C421/97 [1999] ECR 1-3633	Article 110 – Similar goods	Different characteristics of cars were cited to distinguish between similar and non-similar.

@ **Visit the book's companion website to test your knowledge**

❖ Resources include a subject map, revision tip podcasts, downloadable diagrams, MCQ quizzes for each chapter, and a flashcard glossary

❖ www.routledge.com/cw/optimizelawrevision

6 Free Movement of Goods 2: Articles 34–36 TFEU

Revision objectives

Understand the law
- Can you outline the different concepts of non-fiscal barriers to trade?
- Which Articles are applicable here?

Remember the details
- Can you remember the distinction between a QR, an MEQR and a Selling arrangement?
- Can you define each element of the key law?

Reflect critically on areas of debate
- Do you understand how a state may justify a barrier to trade?
- Can you define the concept of non-fiscal barriers accurately and critically discuss in relation to case-law examples?

Contextualise
- Can you relate and compare these concepts to other areas of EU law such as the fiscal barriers to trade?

Apply your skills and knowledge
- Could you apply the relevant cases and legislation in answering a problem scenario?

Chapter Map

Non-fiscal barriers
Article 34

Quantitative restrictions

- '... measures which amount to a total or partial restraint of, according to the circumstances, imports, exports or goods in transit.' *(Geddo v Ente Nazionale Risi)*
- Refers to restrictions on the quantity of imports such as bans and quotas

Measures having equivalent effect to quantitative restrictions (MEQRs)

'All trading rules enacted by member states which are capable of hindering, directly or indirectly, actually or potentially, intra-community trade.' *(Procureur du Roi v Dassonville)*

Distinctly applicable MEQRs

= measures which do not apply equally to domestic and imported goods (see Article 2 of Directive 70/50)

Indistinctly applicable MEQRs

= measures which apply equally to imported and domestic goods (see Article 3 of Directive 70/50 (repealed))
Governed by the presumption of Mutual Recognition (*Cassis de Dijon*)

Selling arrangements

Are not MEQRs as long as:

- they apply to all relevant traders operating within the national territory; and
- they affect in the same manner, in law and in fact, the marketing of domestic products and of those from other Member States (*Keck*).

Article 36 Derogations

- Specifies grounds on which restrictions can be justified.
- Must not constitute:
  - a means of arbitrary discrimination; or
  - a disguised restriction on trade between Member States
  - Must not be disproportionate

Mandatory requirements (Rule of reason)

- Additional grounds recognised by the Court of Justice on which restrictions can be justified.
- Originally established in Cassis de Dijon
- Only available for indistinctly applicable MEQRs
- Must not be disproportionate

Introduction

This chapter considers in detail the Treaty provisions concerning the non-fiscal barriers that may impede the free flow of goods between Member States. A Member State may be concerned about the health risk posed by produce from another state and may wish to impose a ban or quota on such goods. This may be justified if the Member State can prove that such a restriction is necessary and justified. This chapter outlines both successful and failed attempts at such restrictions.

Who is bound by Article 34 TFEU?

The key focus of Article 34 is the Member State itself. Measures adopted by Member States that constitute restrictions on imports and exports will violate the prohibition. The Member State will also be held liable where it has not taken action to stop individuals flouting the rules.

In *Commission v France* (the *Spanish Strawberries* case), the French government was found liable under Article 34 for not taking adequate measures against French farmers, who had, for years, violently sabotaged imports of Spanish strawberries.

The Article 34 prohibition has been widely defined by the CJ and includes measures adopted by public or quasi-public bodies within the Member State concerned. For example, in *R v Royal Pharmaceutical Society of Great Britain, ex parte Association of Pharmaceutical*, Article 34 was applied to measures adopted by the body responsible for regulating the pharmaceutical profession in the UK.

Other examples of such bodies can be seen in cases such as:

❖ *Apple and Pear Development Council v Lewis*; and
❖ *Commission v Ireland*.

Article 34 TFEU: Restrictions on imports

Article 34
'Quantitative restrictions on imports and all measures having equivalent effect shall be prohibited between Member States.'

Quantitative restrictions

Quantative restrictions (QRs) were defined by the CJ in *Geddo v Ente Nazionale Risi*. They are:

'...measures which amount to a total or partial restraint'...of imports, exports or goods in transit'.

The CJ has also identified that, apart from bans on imports, imposed quotas on imports also constitute QRs in violation of Article 34 (e.g. a licensing system that only allows importers to import a specific quantity of a product as in *International Fruit Co (No. 2) v Produktschap voor Groenten*).

Measures having equivalent effect

Measures having equivalent effect (MEQR) cover a wide range of measures that can be regarded as disguised barriers to trade (e.g. restrictions on the labeling or packaging used for a product). The restriction at first appears not to harm imports directly until it becomes obvious that the importer is at a disadvantage because the domestic producer has always abided by such laws and does not need to alter their product accordingly. The classic definitions of an MEQR are as follows:

Directive 70/50

This directive was a transitional measure that is no longer in force in the EU. However, it indicates the Commission's approach to MEQRs and remains instructive in understanding much of the subsequent case law that has developed. The directive divided MEQRs into two groups:

Distinctly applicable measures	Indistinctly applicable measures
❖ These do not apply equally to domestic and imported goods. ❖ Such measures discriminate against imports because they make importation more difficult or costly relative to the domestic product. ❖ One example provided by the Directive is national rules that demand higher standards in respect of imported goods than domestic goods (Article 2 of Directive 70/50).	❖ These measures appear, on their face, to be equally applicable to domestic and imported goods, but the effect of the measures disadvantages imported goods by requiring them to satisfy the state's domestic set of rules for similar products. ❖ These measures cover the marketing of products in the widest sense. ❖ A good example is a national rule that imposes conditions on the packaging or composition of products.

Case precedent – *Walter: Rau Lebensmittelwerke v de Smedt PvbA*

Facts: Belgian statute required all margarine in Belgium to be sold in cubic packages. Although this law was addressed to all margarine producers, irrespective of origin, it had the practical effect of stopping the sale of imports which were packaged differently and protecting domestic producers. The Belgian margarine market had the symptoms of a protected and isolated market: no foreign competition and high prices. The Belgian Government defended the law on the basis of the avoidance of consumer confusion.

Principle: CJ accepted this as a potentially legitimate justification of a MEQR under Article 36 (public policy), but found that it failed the requirement of proportionality (there were better ways of achieving the Belgian Government's objectives).

Application: It is possible for a Member State to implement restrictive rules, but they need to have a proportionate effect on imports.

Dassonville for Procureur du Roi v Benoit and Gustave Dassonville

'All trading rules enacted by Member States which are capable of hindering, directly or indirectly, actually or potentially, intra-Community trade.'

The above definition is very wide, even extending to the potential to hinder trade.

The distinction between these two categories is important due to the fact that the defences available for each category differ.

Distinctly applicable measures can only be justified, if at all, under Article 36 (as is also the case with QRs). Indistinctly applicable measures are treated more leniently: they can be justified either under Article 36 or by reference to 'mandatory requirements'. These are discussed below.

Distinctly applicable MEQRs

The CJ's case law reveals a wide variety of MEQRs that have infringed Article 34 and that which can be classified as distinctly applicable measures. Some examples are set out below:

Restriction	Case	Result
Imposing additional requirements on imported goods	*Firma Denkavit Futtermittel GmbH v Minister für Ernähgrung*	A requirement that imported goods should be inspected was held to breach Article 34 because of the delays in the inspection process and the increased transport costs.
National rules giving preference to domestic goods	*Commission v Ireland* (the *Buy Irish* case)	A campaign by the Irish Goods Council to promote Irish goods was regarded as a MEQR in violation of Article 34 because imports would be likely to be affected by the campaign. The CJ held that consumers were likely to be influenced by a national body (in fact, they were not).
	Commission v Ireland	Irish rules required imported jewellery that incorporated motifs suggesting that they were souvenirs from Ireland (e.g. a shamrock motif) to bear an indication of the country in which it was made and the word 'foreign'. The defence of the Irish Government was that consumers wanted to buy souvenirs that had been made in the country they were visiting and needed such origin-marking to distinguish such items. The CJ held that buyers did not need to know where the particular product came from and hence the rules constituted an MEQR that violated Article 34.
Restricting channels of distribution for imported goods	*Dassonville for Procureur du Roi v Benoit and Gustave Dassonville*	The facts were that Belgian law required goods to carry a certificate of origin issued by the Member State in which they were manufactured. Dassonville imported Scotch whisky into Belgium from France. As it was not importing directly from the UK, the requirement that it should obtain the requisite certificate was onerous: it favoured direct importers from the UK over indirect importers and therefore hampered free trade.

Indistinctly applicable MEQRs

Often, Member States will have rules in place concerning the labelling and/or packaging of goods. These requirements will often result in additional burdens being placed on importers, and hence trade being restricted. This will often arise because the importer must satisfy the regulatory regime that applies to its product in at least two jurisdictions: the importer's state as well as the state into which the product is being imported. In effect, the importer needs two production lines. The competing domestic products, on the other hand, will only have to satisfy the requirements of the domestic regime.

Case precedent – *Keck and Mithouard*

Facts: France had rules in place outlawing the selling of products at a loss.

Principle: This was successfully challenged on the grounds that these rules were not product based but were described as selling arrangements.

Application: The CJ stated that product requirements involved the 'designation, form, size, weight, composition, presentation, labelling [and] packaging' of the product concerned will be regarded as indistinctly applicable MEQR's.

The following cases are examples.

Case	Facts	Result
Verein gegen Unwesen in Handel und Gewerbe Koln v Mars GmbH	A sales promotion in which Mars sold ice cream bars 10% larger than the usual size and marked the wrappers '10%' with a coloured flash on the end of the wrappers (that was deceptively bigger than 10% of the length) was challenged by German consumer authorities. This was on the grounds that it created the impression that the 10% increase was free and the graphical impression created by the flash made the bar seem even bigger. Mars challenged this view.	The CJ accepted that as the bars with these wrappers were being sold throughout the EU they must also be sold in Germany on the basis of the dual burden rule. In arriving at this conclusion, the court concluded that the wrappers were part of the product. The manufacturer would either have to change the wrappers at the border or have a second production line for its German distributors.

Case	Facts	Result
Commission v Ireland (Re Dundalk Water Supply)	Contractors tendering for the contract to supply water to Dundalk were required by the Irish government to supply pipes which complied with 'Irish Standard Mark 188'. This was indistinctly applicable because all pipes, whether Irish or foreign, were expected to reach this standard. Only one manufacturer made such pipes and it was Irish. One contractor's bid was made on the basis of supplying pipes to an international standard but not to this particular Irish standard and was rejected for this reason alone.	The CJ held that the specification constituted a barrier to imported pipes that were appropriate to the contract and was caught. The court went on to point out that while the government could lay down specifications for materials, had they incorporated the words 'or equivalent' after the Irish standard it would not have created a barrier.

Common Pitfalls

Students are not always clear on the distinctions between QRs and MEQRs and between distinctly applicable and indistinctly applicable. It is important to understand these as the defences available to Member States will vary depending on the initial classification of the restriction.

Defences

As noted, it is possible for states to invoke one or more of the derogations from Article 36 TFEU as a potential defence to an alleged breach under Article 34. The derogations in Article 36 may be used as a defence to QRs and MEQRs including both distinctly and indistinctly applicable.

The six derogations on which Member States may rely are:

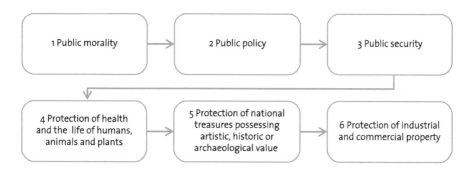

In addition, Article 36 states that the derogations cannot be relied upon if the measure employed by the state constitutes arbitrary discrimination or a disguised restriction on trade. Also, any measure taken by a Member State to achieve the objectives set out in Article 36 must be proportionate.

The following are case illustrations the use of each derogation

R v Thompson

The UK banned the export of silver coins to prevent them from being melted down or destroyed.

There was also a ban in the UK on such coins being melted down or destroyed.

The CJ accepted that the ban stemmed from the need of the state to protect the right to mint coinage, which involved a fundamental interest of the state.

Cullet Leclerc Toulouse

The Leclerc group started selling petrol at prices below those set by French law. A competitor brought proceedings against Leclerc on the basis of the French law. Leclerc argued, and the CJ accepted, that the minimum price law was an infringement of Article 34 as it allowed the authorities to manipulate prices and prevent importers from entering the market. The French government argued that the public policy derogation applied, on account of the threat to public order and security that would result from local retailers if faced with unrestricted competition. The CJ rejected this argument on the basis that the French government had not proved that it could not deal with these threats or possible disruptions using the traditional means at its disposal.

Public policy

R v Henn and Darby

This concerned a UK ban on the import of obscene films and magazines. Although this constituted a QR, Article 36 could be relied upon by the UK:

'it is for each Member State to determine in accordance with its own scale of values and in the form selected by it the requirements of public morality'.

The UK Government was not arbitrarily discriminating against imported goods as there was no lawful trade in such goods in the UK.

Conegate v HM Customs & Excise Commissioners

The UK sought to prevent the import of life-size inflatable 'love-love' dolls from Germany. The difficulty faced by the UK in attempting to invoke the public morality derogation was that the same goods could be lawfully manufactured in the UK.

The CJ held that the derogation was not available to the UK. This meant that the ban arbitrarily discriminated against imported goods.

Public morality

Campus Oil Ltd v Minister for Industry and Energy

Ireland, which is completely dependent on imports for its supplies of petroleum products, required importers to buy 35% of their requirements from a state-owned oil refinery at prices fixed by the Irish Government. The CJ held that this was an MEQR, but it accepted the argument that the restriction was necessary on the grounds of public security. Because of the exceptional importance of petroleum products as an energy source, an interruption of supplies could seriously affect public security.

   The restriction allowed Ireland to maintain its own oil refining capacity and was proportionate demonstrating that any derogation must satisfy this proportionality test.

 Public security

Commission v Greece

The state's claim to exclusive marketing of oil products was not proportionate.

Commission v UK

The CJ decided that the UK ban on poultry products from Member States shortly before Christmas in 1981 was a disguised restriction on trade. The measures had been hastily introduced and timed to coincide with the beginning of the Christmas season. The British Government had also reacted to successful lobbying by local turkey producers who had been concerned about the dramatic increase in the number of turkeys imported from France. There was also no genuine health reason for the measure. The real aim of the restriction was to block, for commercial and economic reasons, imports of poultry products from other Member States, especially France.

Santoz

The Dutch authorities refused to grant authorisation for the import of muesli bars with added vitamins from Germany.

   The CJ accepted that the dearth of scientific evidence about vitamins meant that the Dutch restriction was justified.

 **Protection of health and the life of humans, animals and plants**

It would now appear that the derogation above may also extend to even wider forms of environmental protection.

Case precedent – *PreussenElektra AG v Schhleswag AG*

Facts: German law required electricity distribution undertakings to purchase at fixed minimum prices electricity produced from renewable energy sources in their area of supply in Germany.

Principle: The CJ held that the legislative policy was justified as it was designed to protect the health and life of humans, animals and plants. Moreover, Article 6 of the EC Treaty (now Article 11 of the TFEU) required environmental protection to be integrated into the definition and implementation of this derogation.

Application: This indicates the potential fluidity between the Cassis exceptions and Article 36.

No case has yet been decided under the heading 'protection of national treasures', it was raised by the Italian government in *Commission v Italy* (the '*Italian Art*' case), which was discussed in Chapter 5. However, that case included a financial measure to which Article 36 does not apply.

The sixth derogation, the protection of industrial and commercial property, is a specialised area within EU law. It mainly deals with the extent to which a domestic trader's intellectual property rights such as trademarks and copyright may be employed by that trader to exclude an importing trader's presence in the domestic market.

Essentially, the approach adopted is that the courts will recognise a domestic trader's ownership of intellectual property rights, but will strictly monitor the trader's exercise of these rights to ascertain whether the rights are being improperly used to impede the free movement of goods. A detailed discussion of this derogation is beyond the scope of the course.

Proportionality

It should be remembered that, to escape a finding that Article 34 has been unlawfully violated, not only must the Member State be able to invoke a recognised ground of derogation in Article 36, but it must also act in a proportionate manner. The court has recognised the proportionality principle on numerous occasions. For instance, a blanket ban on fortified foods by the Dutch Government was disproportionate in the absence of a case-by-case assessment of the possible public health effects (*C v Netherlands*). *Campus Oil* and *Commission v Greece* (discussed above) are further examples.

Defences II: The Cassis de Dijon rules

> **Case precedent – *Rewe-Zentral AG v Bundesmonopolverwaltung für Branntwein* (the '*Cassis de Dijon*' case)**

Facts: German law specified a minimum alcohol level of 25% for certain spirits including cassis, a blackcurrant fruit liqueur made in France. The law was indistinctly applicable because it applied equally to domestic and imported liqueurs, but it had the effect of impeding the importation of French cassis which had an alcohol content of between 15% and 20%.

Principle: The CJ accepted that the German requirement amounted to an MEQR, and it was not argued that Article 36 in any way saved the requirement. The CJ articulated two important, contradictory principles in *Cassis*: the presumption of mutual recognition (alternatively referred to as the dual burden rule or the presumption of marketability) and the rule of reason, which have to be balanced against each other.

Application: The case is influential in allowing for States to introduce restrictions beyond those listed in Article 36. The rules can be used by both the state and the importer as a means to extend or challenge restrictions on trade.

The two rules work as follows:

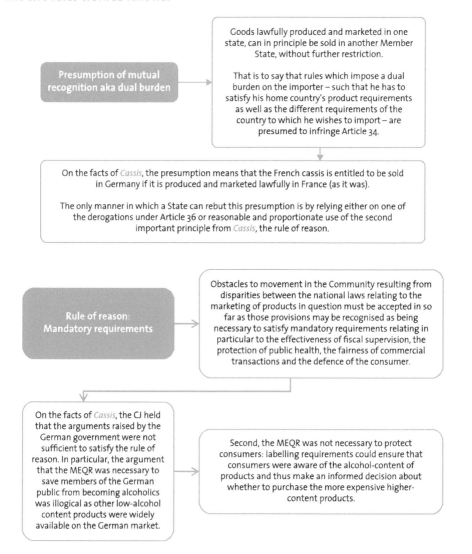

Key cases following *Cassis*

There have been a number of cases where the two principles in *Cassis* have been further developed.

Case	Facts	Result
Commission v Italy (the *'Relabelling of Cocoa Products'* case)	An Italian rule limited the name 'chocolate' to products made with cocoa fats and required chocolate with vegetable fats to be described as 'chocolate substitute'.	The CJ held that this infringed Article 34 as the label 'substitute' would adversely impact on consumer perceptions and thus impede trade. The imported products were lawfully produced and marketed as 'chocolate' in their home countries and there was no significant difference between the two types of chocolate products. The presumption of mutual recognition was not rebutted by any mandatory requirement.
Cinethéque SA v Fédération Nationale des Cinémas Français	A French law that banned the sale or hire of videos of films during the first year of their release was justified as being necessary to encourage the French public to go to the cinema and protect the profitability of cinematographic production.	The rule applied equally to domestic and imported films (it was an indistinctly applicable MEQR) and it was a proportionate means of achieving the objective of protecting cinematographic production.
Commission v Denmark (the *'Disposable Beer Cans'* case)	Laws that required drinks to be produced in standard size containers for recycling.	These were justified on the basis that they proportionally met the objective of protecting the environment.
Schmidberger	Austria allowed a one-day environmental demonstration to temporarily close the Brenner motorway (a major trade route through Austria).	The citizens' fundamental freedom of expression and assembly was accepted by the CJ as a justified restriction on free movement of goods. This was, of course, a further extension of the mandatory requirement category.

Conclusion

Cassis has created a structured manner in which the legitimacy of indistinctly applicable MEQRs may be assessed. However, in practice, *Cassis* had the result that many measures taken by Member States breached the presumption of mutual recognition without the possibility of being saved by a mandatory requirement. Any measure that impacted on the volume of trade in a product was theoretically challengeable. Governments were concerned that the dual-burden principle was effectively undermining the ability of Member States to impose reasonable national measures that were necessary, but may not necessarily be saved by mandatory requirements. A challenge to the Sunday Trading laws in the UK occurred in the following.

Case precedent – *Torfaen Borough Council v B&Q plc*

Facts: British law required most shops to be closed on Sundays. Some DIY stores catering to home decorating consumers breached this law and started to trade on Sundays. In the prosecution of the stores, the defence was that the Sunday trading rules breached Article 34, because imported goods could also not be sold on Sundays, thus impeding trade from Member States.

Principle: The CJ treated the Sunday trading rules as MEQRs, *prima facie* falling within the Article 34 structure, but left it to national courts to decide whether the restriction on trade was necessary and proportionate. The UK courts, not familiar with these concepts, arrived at differing conclusions. The issue was settled in *Stoke-on-Trent and Norwich City Councils v B & Q plc*, in which the rules were found to be justified and proportionate. Sunday trading rules did affect trade volume but they affected domestic goods and imports alike.

Application: This appeared to be an undue restriction on the ability of Member States to create trading rules.

The decision of the CJ in *Keck* responded to this concern and was an attempt by the CJ to distinguish between indistinctly applicable measures that hinder trade between Member States (which were unlawful unless justified by Article 36 or the mandatory requirements) and indistinctly applicable measures that had an effect on the overall volume of trade, but did not affect imports more than domestic products. In *Keck*, the CJ labelled the latter category 'selling arrangements' and decided that these arrangements were not even MEQRs, such that Article 34 was not engaged at the outset.

Case precedent – *Keck and Mithouard*

Facts: That Keck and Mithouard sold goods at a loss in contravention of French law. When they were prosecuted, the defence they raised was that the law itself contravened Article 34 as it constituted an indistinctly applicable MEQR. The law deprived them of a method of promoting their goods and thus reduced the volume of sales of goods imported by them into France.

Principle: The EU expressly held that it wanted to clarify the law in regard to Article 34 in view of the 'increasing tendency of traders' to employ Article 34 to argue that any restriction on their commercial freedom was unlawful. The main distinction that the court endorsed was that referred to earlier, between product requirements and selling arrangements.

Application: *Cassis* will apply to product requirements but not to selling arrangements, provided the selling arrangements:

(a) apply to all affected traders operating within the national territory; and
(b) affect in the same manner in law and in fact the marketing of domestic and imported products.

Selling arrangements

As stated the best example of an indistinctly applicable MEQR was a product requirement, such as the restriction in issue in the *Cassis* case. These will inevitably be subject to, and in breach of, Article 34.

In contrast, selling arrangements are those rules that concern who sells the product and when, where and how he goes about it; not the physical characteristics of the goods themselves.

Selling arrangements applying equally in law and in fact fall outside the Article 34 structure because they have the same effect in practice on both domestic goods and imports.

Outside Article 34

Tankstation 't Heukste vof and JBE Boermans

❖ Dutch rules regarding the closure of all petrol stations at night, and which applied to all traders operating in the national territory, were not caught by Article 34. The rules affected domestic and foreign producers in the same way in law and fact.

Punto Casa SpA v Sindaco del Commune di Capena and others
> ❖ A similar decision was reached with regard to Sunday trading rules in Italy.

Herbert Karner Industrie – Auktionen GmbH v Troostwijk GmbH
> ❖ An Austrian restriction on the advertising of auctions of goods bought from insolvent firms, which had the aim of preventing consumers being given a misleading impression about potential prices, was seen as a selling arrangement and not caught by Article 34.

Inside Article 34

Konsumentombudsmannen (KO) v De Agostini (Svenska) Förlag AB
> ❖ The case concerned a Swedish ban on television advertising directed at children under 12 years old and a ban on misleading advertisements for skincare products and detergents. The court accepted that these restrictions were selling arrangements, but went on to consider whether the arrangement complied with the two requirements set out above. The first requirement was satisfied: the ban applied to all traders operating within the territory.
>
> ❖ But the CJ held that the second requirement – that the ban must affect all traders in the same manner in law and fact – may not be satisfied. The outright ban on a manner of promoting a product may have a greater impact on products from other Member States and De Agostini had stated that television promotion was the only effective manner of penetrating the Swedish market. The CJ decided to leave the determination of whether the ban discriminated in fact against imported products to the national court, but the point is that if discrimination did exist, the arrangement would fall to be considered under the Article 34 regime.

Konsumentombudsmannen v Gourmet International Products Aktiebolag

❖ The Swedish government restricted the advertising of alcoholic drinks on radio and TV and in magazines and other publications, unless the magazine was distributed solely at the point of sale of the beverage. Gourmet published a magazine that reached members of the public and that contained advertisements for alcohol in breach of the Swedish legislation. The CJ held that this type of selling arrangement had to be considered within the Article 34 structure of analysis.

❖ The arrangement impeded access by foreign producers to the alcoholic beverage market more than domestic producers because consumers would be more familiar with the domestic goods. So the arrangement constituted an indistinctly applicable MEQR. The Swedish Government's argument that the MEQR was justifiable in terms of the public health derogation in Article 36 was left for the national court to determine.

Vereinigte Familiapress Zeitungsverlags und Vertreibs GmbH v Heinrich Bauer Verlag

❖ The Austrian Unfair Competition Act did not allow the sale of newspapers and magazines which contained competitions giving big money prizes. Although aimed at enhancing the diversity of the press by protecting journals unable to afford such sales promotions the CJ decided that this could not be a selling arrangement as it was based upon the actual content of the journals. As such competitions formed an integral part of the journal it failed the dual burden test and was caught by Article 34.

❖ However the CJ did go on to acknowledge that the diversity of the press was a general principle of community law and a mandatory requirement which could override Article 34. It was left to the national court to decide whether the Austrian law was a proportionate method of ensuring press plurality or whether it could be achieved less restrictively.

Article 35 TFEU: Restrictions on exports

Article 35 is the mirror image of Article 34 except that the prohibition is directed at exports and not imports. It prohibits QRs and MEQRs in relation to exports. There is much less case law in regard to Article 35 than Article 34, mainly because Member States generally encourage exports in their own interests.

The same structure of analysis will apply to Article 35 as has been discussed at length with respect to Article 34. There is one important exception, however. Article 35 strikes at QRs – the export ban on silver coins in Thompson, for example – and distinctly applicable MEQRs. An indistinctly applicable MEQR will not breach Article 35. The reason for this difference is that the rationale for restricting indistinctly applicable measures – that the importer will otherwise be forced to comply with two sets of rules as to his product – does not apply in the case of exports. An exporter only has to comply with the product requirements of one country. Thus, Article 35 prohibits only MEQRs that are distinctly applicable, or, stated differently, directly discriminatory.

This position was confirmed in *Groenveld BV v Produktschap voor Vee en Vlees*. Dutch law prohibited all manufacturers of meat products from having horsemeat in stock, in order to ensure that horsemeat would not be exported by accident to countries where it is banned. This is an example of an indistinctly applicable measure, because it applies equally to all meat producers. The CJ held that such a measure was not regulated by Article 35, even though it might have the effect of restricting exports of meat. Article 35 will only apply to measures that have 'as their specific object or effect the restriction on the patterns of export and thereby the establishment of a difference in treatment between the domestic trade of a Member State and its export trade'.

As with Article 34, if a QR or a distinctly applicable MEQR exists such that there is a *prima facie* violation of Article 35, the Member State may seek to argue that the derogations set out in Article 36 apply. The two principles set out in *Cassis* do not apply to Article 35.

Sample question

Dali SA is a Spanish manufacturer of crayons and pencils. As part of their marketing campaigns, they describe their products as 'organic' and 'environmentally friendly' pointing out the fact that the products use recycled materials and have minimum packaging. The company has been very successful in establishing themselves in the Spanish, French and Italian markets where they are well known for their product quality and inventive advertising.

Recently, a decision has been reached to launch their range in the UK and Holland. However, lawyers working for Dali have identified a number of issues which may cause the company problems in selling in these new markets.

First, in the UK, a consumer statute prevents products from being marketed using the word 'organic' as this has a standard meaning in the UK and the use of the word is subject to approval by a government agency. Such approval for Dali could take up to six to 12 months before being granted. The company is concerned as both their advertising campaigns and their packaging feature this word heavily.

In addition, Dutch law has recently banned certain types of materials including those recycled ones used by Dali in their manufacturing processes. This is due to a recent health scare in Holland which has been attributed to the leaking of these materials into the food chain.

Dali is concerned that these rules will hinder them in their drive to expand and have sought your legal advice.

Advise Dali.

Suggested solution

This area of law involves a clear identification into whether the law is a QR, MEQR or SA. This will be crucial to your analysis of the problem. It is also important to identify the issues in the question. These are:

UK
- The ban on the use of the word organic in their advertising campaigns
- The ban on the use of the word organic on the packaging

Holland
- The ban on the use of certain recycled materials in their products

Issue 1 – Advertising campaign

The key case to start with is *Keck*, which established the concept of the 'selling arrangement'.

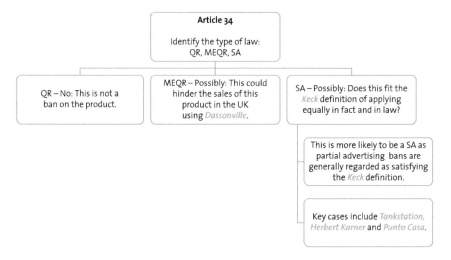

Conclusion

As Dali could advertise in many other ways which do not involve the use of the word organic, then it is best argued that this is about selling rather than the product and is thus a selling arrangement.

Issue 2 – Packaging

As a rough guide, rules which involve importers having to change their product are more likely to be MEQRs rather than SAs.

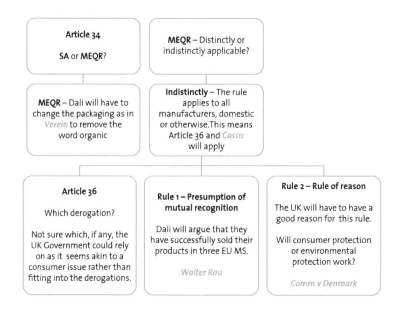

Conclusion

Unless the UK can provide a very good justification for the rule, it is arguable that Dali will succeed using the presumption of mutual recognition as the UK has failed to displace this.

Issue 3 – Ban on recycled materials

This is an issue which can cause problems for students. Many will simply see the word ban and argue that this is a QR under Article 34. This is not correct as it is not the products that have been banned, as was the case in *Conegate*, but instead, the raw materials; Dali could remove these and then sell their products without the offending part. This clearly has cost implications for them and might not be practicable. How do we deal with this issue?

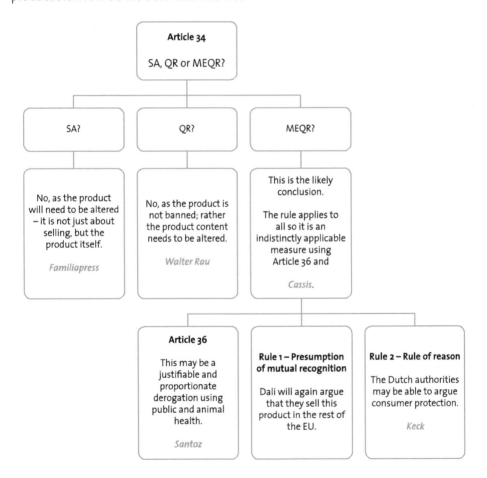

Conclusion

It seems to be the case that in the event of a genuine health scare, the Dutch Government could rely on Article 36 and even the second *Cassis* rule. This would, however, need to be a proportionate response to the issue.

Table of key cases refered to in this chapter

Case name	Area of law	Principle
Apple and Pear Development Council v Lewis C222/82 [1983] ECR 4083	Public bodies under Article 34	This was judged as falling within Article 34.
C v Netherlands C41/02 [2004] ECR 1-11375	Proportionality	The doctrine was recognised in conjunction with Article 36.
Campus Oil Ltd v Minister for Industry and Energy AC72/83 [1984] ECR 2727	Article 36	This fell within the public security defence.
Cinethéque SA v Fédération Nationale des Cinémas Français C60 & 61/84 [1985] ECR 2605	*Cassis* rules	Protecting cinema culture was an acceptable mandatory requirement.
Commission v Denmark (the '*Disposable Beer Cans*' case) C302/86 [1988] ECR 4607	*Cassis* rules	Recycling fell within the rule of reason.
Commission v France (the '*Spanish Strawberries*' case) C265/95 [1997] ECR I-6959	Public bodies under Article 34	The French Government was found liable for inaction against French farmers.
Commission v Greece C347/88 [1990] ECR I-4747	Article 36	The public security defence failed.
Commission v Ireland (the '*Buy Irish*' case) 249/81 [1982] ECR 4005	Public bodies under Article 34	A 'buy Irish' campaign was illegal under Article 34.
Commission v Ireland (Re Dundalk Water Supply) Case 45/87 [1988] ECR 4929	Indistinctly applicable MEQRs	The technical specification for water pipes was an MEQR.
Commission v Ireland (the '*Irish Souvenirs*' case) C113/80 [1981] ECR 1625	Distinctly applicable MEQRs	Insisting that souvenirs be made in Ireland was deemed to be an MEQR.
Commission v Italy (the '*Relabelling of Cocoa Products*' case) C14/00 [2003] ECR I-513	*Cassis* rules	The requirement of the label 'chocolate substitute' was an MEQR.
Commission v UK (the '*Imports of Poultry Meat*' case) C40/82 [1982] ECR 2793	Article 36	The defence failed here.

Conegate v HM Customs & Excise Commissioners C121/85 [1986] ECR 1007	Article 36	The restriction on imports was a breach of Article 34.
Cullet Leclerc Toulouse C231/83 [1985] ECR 305	Article 36	Fell outside the public policy defence.
Dassonville for Procureur du Roi v Benoit and Gustave Dassonville C8/74 [1974] ECR 837	MEQRs	This contains the definition of an MEQR.
Firma Denkavit Futtermittel GmbH v Minister für Ernähgrung C251/78 [1979] ECR 3369	Distinctly applicable MEQRs	An inspection was a breach of Article 34.
Geddo v Ente Nazionale Risi C2/73 [1973] ECR 865	Quantitative restrictions	This case contains the definition of a QR.
Groenveld BV v Produktschap voor Vee en Vlees C15/7 [1979] ECR 3409	Article 35	Only distinctly applicable MEQRs fall under this article.
Herbert Karner Industrie – Auktionen GmbH v Troostwijk GmbH C71/02 [2004] 2 CMLR 75	Selling arrangements	Rules on auctions fell within SA.
International Fruit Co (No. 2) v Produktschap voor Groenten C51–4/71 [1971] ECR 1107	Quantitative restrictions	Quotas also fall within Article 34.
Keck and Mithouard C267 & 268/91 [1993] ECR I-6097	Indistinctly applicable MEQRs and selling arrangements	Selling at a loss fell outside Article 34.
Konsumentombudsmannen (KO) v De Agostini (Svenska) Förlag AB C34–36/95 [1997] ECR I-3843	Selling arrangements	A ban on advertising to children was a potential MEQR.
Konsumentombudsmannen v Gourmet International Products Aktiebolag C405/98 [2001] ECR I-1795	Selling arrangements	The Swedish Government's argument that the MEQR was justifiable in terms of the public health derogation in Article 36 was left for the national court to determine.

Case name	Area of law	Principle
PreussenElektra AG v Schhleswag AG C379/98 [2001] ECR I-2099	Article 36	The legislative policy was justified under Article 36.
Punto Casa SpA v Sindaco del Commune di Capena and others C69 & 258/93 [1994] ECR I-2355	Selling arrangements	Sunday trading rules were MEQRs.
R v Henn and Darby C34/79 [1979] ECR 3795	Quantitative restrictions	A ban on the importation of pornography was OK under Article 36.
R v Royal Pharmaceutical Society of Great Britain, ex parte Association of Pharmaceutical Importers C266 & 267/87 [1989] ECR 1295	Public bodies under Article 34	This body regulated the pharmaceutical industry in the UK and fell within Article 34.
R v Thompson C7/78 [1978] ECR 2247	Article 36	Fell within the public policy defence.
Rewe-Zentral AG v Bundesmonopolverwaltung für Branntwein (the '*Cassis de Dijon*' case) C120/78 [1979] ECR 649	*Cassis* rules	The case which established the two key rules.
Santoz C174/82 [1983] ECR 2445	Article 36	The protection of health of animals argument was successful.
Schmidberger C112/00 [2003] ECR 1-5659	*Cassis* rules	The citizens' fundamental freedom of expression and assembly was accepted by the CJ as a justified restriction on free movement of goods.
Tankstation 't Heukste vof and JBE Boermans C401 & 402/92 [1994] ECR I-2199	Selling arrangements	The arrangements for the sale of petrol was an SA.
Torfaen Borough Council v B & Q plc C145/88 [1989] ECR 3851	Selling arrangements	Sunday trading rules initially fell within SA.
Walter: Rau Lebensmittelwerke v de Smedt PvbA C261/81 [1982] ECR 3961	MEQRs	A restriction on packaging of margarine was in breach of Article 34.

Verein gegen Unwesen in Handel und Gewerbe Koln v Mars GmbH C470/93 [1995] ECR 1	Indistinctly applicable MEQRs	Having to change the packaging on a Mars Bar was a restriction of trade.
Vereinigte Familiapress Zeitungsverlags und Vertreibs GmbH v Heinrich Bauer Verlag C368/95 [1997] ECR1-3689	Selling arrangements	Having to change magazine content was an MEQR.

@ Visit the book's companion website to test your knowledge

❖ Resources include a subject map, revision tip podcasts, downloadable diagrams, MCQ quizzes for each chapter, and a flashcard glossary

❖ www.routledge.com/cw/optimizelawrevision

7

Free Movement of Persons

Revision objectives

Understand the law
- Can you outline the key law relating to free movement of persons?
- What is the key article?

Remember the details
- Can you remember the differences between workers and citizens?
- Why is this distinction important?

Reflect critically on areas of debate
- Do you understand the circumstances in which a state may exclude an individual?
- Can you analyse and support this with case examples?

Contextualise
- Can you relate and compare these concepts to other areas of EU law such as free movement of goods?

Apply your skills and knowledge
- Could you produce a coherent essay argument on this topic?

Chapter Map

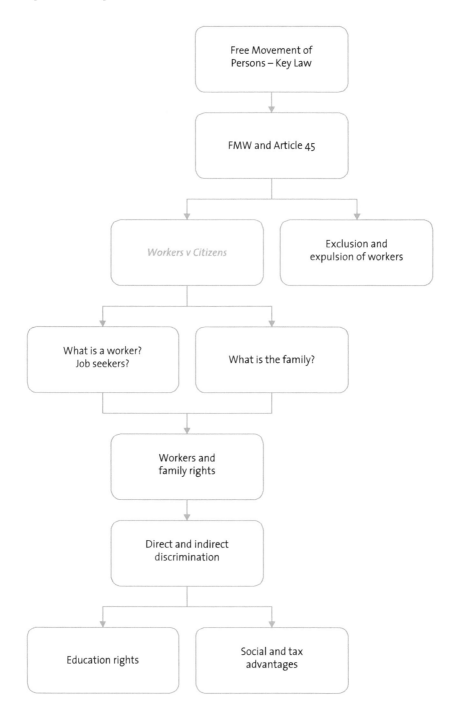

Free Movement of
Persons – Key Law

FMW and Article 45

Workers v Citizens

Exclusion and
expulsion of workers

What is a worker?
Job seekers?

What is the family?

Workers and
family rights

Direct and indirect
discrimination

Education rights

Social and tax
advantages

Introduction

Free movement of persons within the Union is a key aim of the Treaties and one of the four essential freedoms of the EU internal market as evidenced by Article 3 TOTEU. However, this area has also given rise to concern by Member States who fear that they have lost control of their borders and have little say over who enters and leaves. This tension is reflected in the EU law itself which seeks to broadly state the rights of both citizens and Member States to achieve a balance between free movement and on the one hand and Member State limitations on the other.

This chapter will focus mostly on workers rights' as this was the primary focus in the original 1957 EEC Treaty. However, there will also be a review of the wider law on citizens post Maastricht, which has expanded the whole concept of free movement.

Free movement rights – The key law

Progression of the Law over Time

EEC Treaty 1957
* Article 45 (ex 39)
* Right of Free Movement of Workers established

Directive 64/221
* Exclusion and expulsion of workers by Member States
* Now part of Directive 2004/38

Regulation 1612/68
* Introduced rights for workers families and further rights for workers
* Now incorporated into the new Directive 2004/38 and new Regulation 492/2011

Directive 2004/38
* Incorporated rights from Directive 64/221 and Regulation 1612/68
* Expanded concept of free movement
* Covers families, students, citizens etc.

Directive 2005/36
* Recognition of professional qualifications

Regulation 492/2011
* Confers rights of equal treatment, residence, and also specific rights that can be enjoyed by workers and their family member

Aim Higher

You should aim to learn the key parts of the law above and understand when to apply and use them. For example, most problem style questions will involve you applying the base article and then any relevant secondary legislation.

This chapter will provide outlines of the key Articles.

Workers v citizens

Originally, the purpose of conferring free movement rights on workers was economic: to ensure that the economically active were able to move throughout the Union to locations where their labour was needed to satisfy the demand for employment. However, Article 18 TFEU establishes the broader principle of non-discrimination on grounds of nationality: it guarantees the right of the individual worker to be free from discrimination on account of nationality and seeks to raise the EU national's standard of living and quality of life by securing work and residency in another Member State. This builds on the introduction of the citizenship concept in the Maastricht Treaty.

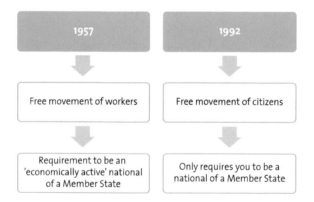

Free movement of workers

The key provision relating to workers is Article 45 TFEU, which provides as follows:

Article 45 TFEU

'1. Freedom of movement for workers shall be secured within the Union.
2. Such freedom of movement shall entail the abolition of any discrimination based on nationality between workers of the Member States as

regards employment, remuneration and other conditions of work and employment.

3. It shall entail the right, subject to limitations justified on grounds of public policy, public security or public health:

   (a) to accept offers of employment actually made;

   (b) to move freely within the territory of Member States for this purpose;

   (c) to stay in a Member State for the purpose of employment in accordance with the provisions governing the employment of nationals of that State laid down by law, regulation or administrative action; and

   (d) to remain in the territory of a Member State after having been employed in that State, subject to conditions which shall be embodied in regulations to be drawn up by the Commission.

4. The provisions of this Article shall not apply to employment in the public service.'

What is a worker?

At present, the basis of free movement has changed to one of EU citizenship. However, if citizens wish to remain in the host State for longer than three months they must still demonstrate that they will not be an economic burden on the host state. To do this they must either possess sufficient resources or be economically active as a worker or self-employed.

Case precedent – *Hoekstra (née Unger) v Bestuur der Bedrijfsvereniging voor Detailhandel en Ambachten*

Facts: This concerned the availability of social security for migrant workers in Germany.

Principle: The CJ held that it had the ultimate authority to define the meaning and scope of the term 'worker', and that it would interpret the term broadly.

Application: Ensures that the definition is consistent across Member States so that the free movement rules are not frustrated.

Article 45 does not define what a worker is: it has been left to the court to determine the approach as in the following cases.

The key case on defining workers is *Lawrie-Blum v Land Baden-Wurttemberg*. A worker must fulfil the following three criteria:

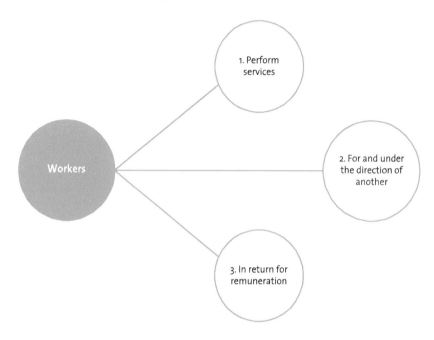

The case concerned a British national who went to the University of Freiburg to train to be a teacher. The German authorities claimed she was not a worker because, although paid for a few hours teaching each week, she was, in reality, training. The key issue was whether a trainee teacher participating in the preparatory stage was a 'worker' under Article 45. The CJ held that a trainee teacher was a worker for the purposes of Community law, as she would fulfil the requirements of the three-part test during the course of training.

The court has defined the concept of worker widely.

Levin v Staatssecretaris van Justitie
- ❖ Facts: Part-time chambermaid
- ❖ Principle: A worker as not ancillary or marginal

Kempf v Staatssecretaris van Justitie
- ❖ Facts: Part-time music teacher, in receipt of benefits
- ❖ Principle: A worker as pursuing a genuine and effective activity

*Walrave & Koch
v Association
Union Cycliste
Internationale*

{
❖ Facts: Pace setters in a cycle race
❖ Principle: Also workers
}

*Steymann v
Staatssecretaris
van Justitie*

{
❖ Facts: Member of a religious community carrying out odd jobs
❖ Principle: Important economic service to the community
}

*Bettray v
Staatsecretaris
van Justitie*

{
❖ Facts: Worked in a drug rehabilitation unit
❖ Principle: However, deemed not to be a worker as the work was ancillary to the main purpose, the recovery and rehabilitation of Bettray
}

New principles have developed with new case law

Up for Debate

Do you think the approach adopted by the courts in the above cases is correct? Or, is the definition of a worker so wide as to be meaningless? (Wyatt and Dashwood's *European Union Law* (6th edn) has a good discussion on this area on starting on p. 503.)

Job seekers

This has been an area of contention as Member States are understandably reluctant to allow individuals to enter without the guarantee of employment for fear of them becoming a drain on state resources. At the same time, it is important to allow workers to move to seek work in states, which are economically buoyant and offering jobs. The court has reached the following compromise.

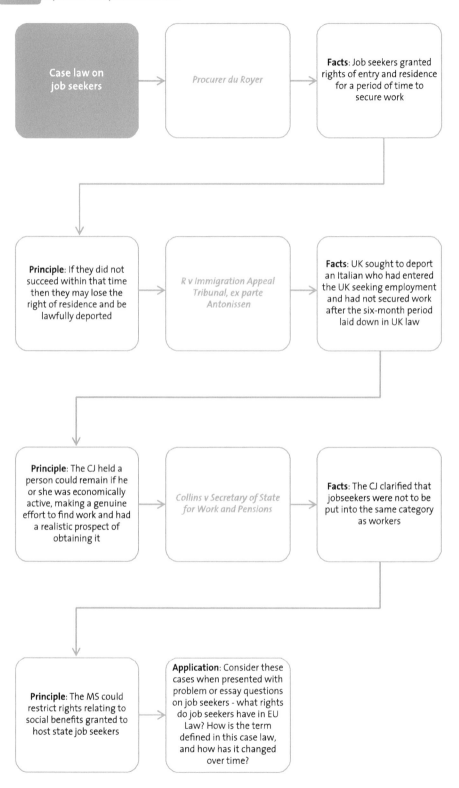

Case law on job seekers → *Procurer du Royer* → **Facts**: Job seekers granted rights of entry and residence for a period of time to secure work

Principle: If they did not succeed within that time then they may lose the right of residence and be lawfully deported → *R v Immigration Appeal Tribunal, ex parte Antonissen* → **Facts**: UK sought to deport an Italian who had entered the UK seeking employment and had not secured work after the six-month period laid down in UK law

Principle: The CJ held a person could remain if he or she was economically active, making a genuine effort to find work and had a realistic prospect of obtaining it → *Collins v Secretary of State for Work and Pensions* → **Facts**: The CJ clarified that jobseekers were not to be put into the same category as workers

Principle: The MS could restrict rights relating to social benefits granted to host state job seekers → **Application**: Consider these cases when presented with problem or essay questions on job seekers - what rights do job seekers have in EU Law? How is the term defined in this case law, and how has it changed over time?

Workers' families

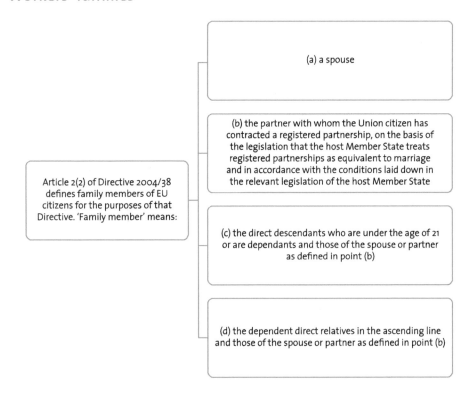

Article 2(2) of Directive 2004/38 defines family members of EU citizens for the purposes of that Directive. 'Family member' means:

(a) a spouse

(b) the partner with whom the Union citizen has contracted a registered partnership, on the basis of the legislation that the host Member State treats registered partnerships as equivalent to marriage and in accordance with the conditions laid down in the relevant legislation of the host Member State

(c) the direct descendants who are under the age of 21 or are dependants and those of the spouse or partner as defined in point (b)

(d) the dependent direct relatives in the ascending line and those of the spouse or partner as defined in point (b)

Note that part (b) above allows for registered partners in the state into which the worker plus partner is intending to enter.

At present, there are only a handful of Member States that recognise registered partnerships as equivalent to marriage. So the rights for free movement for registered partners wanting equivalent status are limited to those States and the registered partner acquires only those rights that are granted to such status by both the home and host State.

In *Netherlands State v Reed*, Ms Reed claimed the right to reside in Holland when she was not herself a worker and was not married to her English partner, who was a worker, with whom she resided. The CJ held that the term 'spouse' was confined to persons married to workers. Accordingly, the CJ ruled that an unmarried partner could not claim rights as a 'spouse' under Article 10 of the Regulation. However, Reed was successful in arguing that Article 7(2) of the Regulation applied because Dutch law allowed nationals to have living with them in Holland their non-national, non-marital partners and that this right constituted a 'social advantage' which should be available to other EU nationals working in the Netherlands (see below on Article 7(2)).

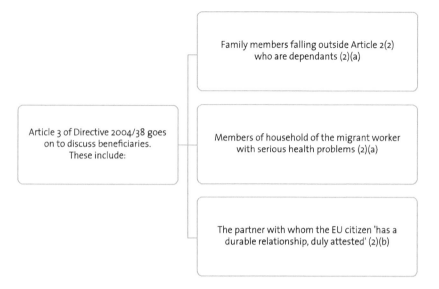

The legislation provides no definition of 'dependant' but in *Jia v Migrationjverket*, the court defined a 'dependant' as someone needing the:

> 'material support [of an EU citizen] in order to meet their essential needs in the State of origin . . . or the State from which they have come at the time when they apply to join that Community national'.

Aim Higher

Consider the reasons for having such expansive laws relating to workers families? How does this support the aim of free movement?

Divorce and separation

This has caused problems due to the fact that if the marriage between an EU national and a non-EU national breaks down, the question of what to do with the non-EU national remains.

The law pre- and post–2004 is indicative of changing attitudes.

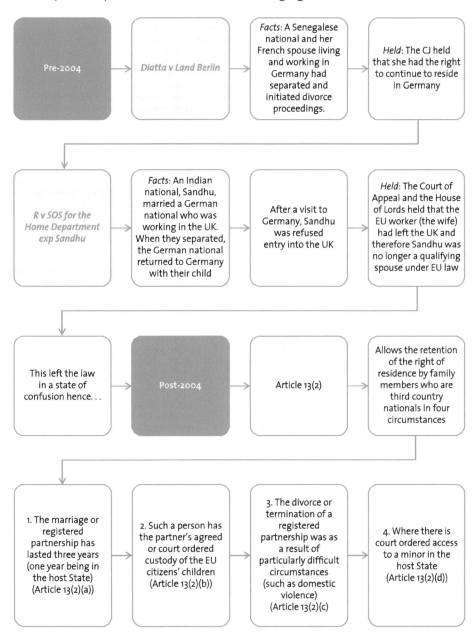

Workers and family rights

It is often the case that the migrant worker will wish to travel with their family members. The rules for these have developed over time so that the family of the worker should also be treated without discrimination with the aim of obtaining equal treatment.

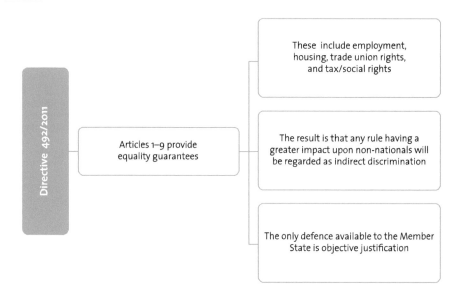

The following diagram illustrates the key law contained in the most pertinent legislation relating to worker's families.

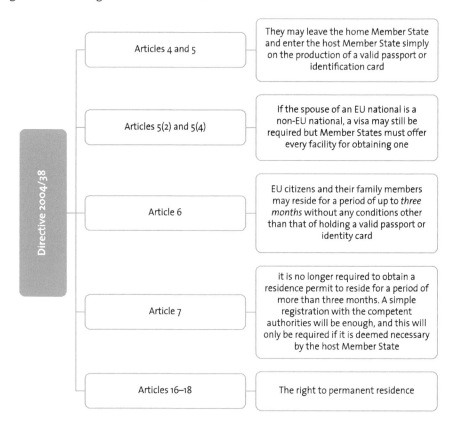

Direct discrimination

Legal if within the public employment derogation contained in Art 45(4)

- Allows Member States to deny or restrict access to employment in the 'public service' on grounds of a worker's nationality. Thus political posts and other sensitive public service posts may be restricted to nationals.
- *Belgian Public Employees*: This case considered the question of whether unskilled workers, nurses, railway workers, architects and others employed by the Belgian government were public employees.
  The CJ defined 'public service' posts as those involving 'the exercise of power conferred by public law' where there was a 'responsibility for safeguarding the general interests of the State'.
  The CJ held that most of the workers were not public employees because they did not exercise public law powers.
- Nurses in public hospitals do not satisfy this test (*Commission v France* (the *Nurses* case)).
  - Nor do trainee schoolteachers (*Lawrie-Blum*).

Not legal if outside this derogation

- *Commission v France (French Merchant Seamen)*

  This concerned Article 4 of Regulation 1612/68 (now Article 4 of Regulation 492/2011) prohibiting national measures restricting the employment of nationals of other Member States by number or percentage.
  The French provision in issue imposed an overall ratio of three French to one non-French national on ships of the merchant fleet.
  By refusing to amend the provision France was held to be in breach of EU law.

Indirect discrimination

Legal if proportionate and objectively justifiable

- *Groener v Ministry for Education*
- The operation of Article 3(1) of Regulation 1612/68 (now Article 3(1)of Regulation 492/2011) arose for consideration. Article 3(1) prohibits discrimination against non-nationals except for the imposition of indirectly discriminatory conditions of eligibility for employment relating to linguistic knowledge, provided that the knowledge is required 'by reason of the post to be filled'.
- *Groener*, a Dutch art teacher was refused an appointment as a lecturer in an Irish vocational school because she did not speak Irish (*Gaeilge*). This was not a requirement of the job since the teaching of art in those schools was conducted in English, but was rather aimed at continuing the language as an aspect of government cultural policy.
- The CJ held that the requirement did indirectly discriminate (not many non-Irish workers spoke Irish), but that the language requirement was not disproportionate to the policy objective and, therefore, was compatible with Regulation 1612/68.

Not legal if no objective justification

- *Württembergische Milchverwertung-Südmilch-AG v Salvatore Ugliola.*
- Indirect discrimination was found where an Italian who had performed military service in the Italian army was working in Germany. His employer conferred seniority to persons for having served in the German army. Ugliola argued that non-Germans were unlikely to serve in that army and that he was therefore subjected to indirect discrimination on the ground of nationality.
- The CJ agreed and held there was no objective justification for the seniority rule.

Workers access to social and tax advantages

Article 7(2) of Regulation 492/2011 provides that 'workers' are entitled to the same 'social and tax advantages'. In other words, non-national workers from Member States are guaranteed the same social and tax advantages as national workers. The CJ has interpreted the provision expansively in order to confer a wide range of benefits upon both workers and their families.

In *Ministère Public v Even*, the CJ held that 'social advantages' are:

> . . . those which, whether or not linked to a contract of employment, are generally granted to workers primarily because of their objective status as workers or by virtue of the mere fact of their residence on the national territory.

These include:

Special fare reduction on railways to large families	❖ *Cristini v SNCF*
Discretionary childbirth loans	❖ *Reina v Landeskreditbank Baden-Württemberg*
Minimum income allowance	❖ *Hoeckx v Centre Public d'Aide Sociale de Kalmthout*
The right to have a foreign partner install themselves in the Member State where the national law allows such a right to its own nationals	❖ *Netherlands State v Reed*

Funeral expenses
benefits { ❖ *O'Flynn v Adjudication Officer*

Right of family members to take up employment

Article 23 of Directive 2004/38 provides that irrespective of nationality, family members of EU citizen who have the right of residence or permanent residence in the Member State shall be entitled to take up employment or self-employment there. It replaced similar right that was conferred by Article 11 of Regulation 1612/68. It should be noted that the right extends to all family members.

Case precedent – *Gül v Regierungspräsident Düsseldorf*

Facts: Gül was a Turkish-Cypriot had qualified as a medical practitioner at Istanbul University. He had married an English hairdresser who was working in Germany. Gül had worked in Germany on a temporary basis for five years and then applied for permanent authorisation to practice in Germany. He was refused on the basis of his nationality and sought to annul the decision.

Principle: The CJ held that as long as he had qualifications and diplomas that were sufficient to comply with German legislation and any specific rules applicable to his profession in Germany; he was entitled under Article 11 of Regulation 1612/68 to practise in Germany because he was a spouse of a 'worker'. It was not necessary that he be an EU national himself.

Application: Member States cannot arbitrarily deny employment opportunities to the family members of migrant workers.

Application: ensures that the definition is consistent across Member States so that the free movement rules are not frustrated.

Up for Debate

What are the political challenges that may arise from an expansive EU approach to allowing workers and their families the right to enter other states, access social and tax advantages and take up work?

Education for workers and their families

Regulation 492/2011 confers the right of equal access to certain kinds of training for workers and the right of broader access to education for their families:

1. Article 7(3) provides that workers have a right of equal access to training in vocational schools and retraining centres.
2. Article 10 provides that children of workers have the same right of entitlement to general education, apprenticeship and vocational training courses as nationals of the Member State.

Within the confines of this definition a worker must be given equal access to such schools, including the imposition of the same level of fees and entry requirements. This might be thought to seriously limit access to education for workers, but this consequence has been largely avoided by the CJ's recourse to Article 7(2) of what is now Regulation 492/2011 and its view that access to education is a 'social advantage'.

By comparison, the CJ has given Article 10 of Regulation 492/2011 (formerly Article 12 of Regulation 1612/68) a wide interpretation, so that it covers 'any form of education' including a university course in economics and advanced vocational training at a tech).

Thus, access to these educational establishments for children of workers resident in another Member State must be on terms equal to that of nationals of the host State.

The more difficult question has been the extent to which these provisions cover the award of grants, rather than simply equal access to educational courses. The position is clearer in relation to Article 10 of Regulation 492/2011.

Case precedent – *Casagrande v Landeshauptstadt München*

Facts: The child of a worker applied for a study grant that was paid to German nationals in similar circumstances.

Principle: The CJ stated that Article 12 of Regulation 1612/68 (now Article 10 of Regulation 492/2011) covers 'any general measures intended to facilitate educational attendance' and thus the grant was payable.

Application: Children of migrant workers are entitled to the same educational opportunities as nationals.

A difficult question which has progressed through the CJ has been access of workers to grants for study under Article 7 of the Regulation.

Lair v Universitat

- This national who had worked intermittently for five years in Germany, then began to study and applied for a maintenance grant.
- The CJ held that a worker who gives up work voluntarily to undertake a course of study in the host Member State must show a link between their previous employment and the later studies in order to qualify for a grant under Article 7(2).

Brown v Secretary of State for Scotland

- The claimant held dual British/French nationality and had completed his schooling in France. He was accepted by a British University to study electrical engineering, but before the course began he undertook an eight-month work placement in Scotland for which a place in a university course was a prerequisite.
- He then applied for a student maintenance grant as a worker under Article 7(2) of Regulation 1612/68 (now Article 7(2) of Regulation 492/2011).
- The CJ held that, although he was engaged in work of a genuine and non-ancillary nature, he could not rely on Article 7(2) because the work was obtained for the purpose of, or incidental to, studies and not in preparation for further employment. Work that is obtained solely as a means of taking up later studies does not qualify a worker for a grant under Article 7(2) of the Regulation.

Maria Martinez Sala v Freistaat Bayern

- This cases concerning welfare benefits held that if EU citizens are lawfully resident in a Member State, they have the right to equal treatment under Article 18 TFEU in all fields covered by the Treaties.

Grzelczyk v Centre Public d'Aide Sociale

- A French student studying in Belgium to claim payment of a minimex (a guaranteed minimum income) by the Belgian state.

R (Bidar) v London Borough of Ealing

- Bidar was entitled to a subsidised loan for higher education in the UK because, although a French national, he had not moved to the UK for a higher educational course. Rather, he had completed his secondary education in the UK while residing with his grandmother, and was integrated into the host society.
- Even though he was not economically active, he could nonetheless, as a citizen of the EU, rely upon Article 18 TFEU once he had been lawfully resident in the UK 'for a certain period of time . . .'.

D'Hoop v Office National de l'Emploi

- A Belgian student sought unemployment benefit from her own national government, after her university studies and pending her first job, on the basis of being an EU worker and a citizen of the EU. She had not in fact completed all her education in Belgium as required by Belgium legislation in conformity with EU law, as she had undertaken secondary education in France.
- The CJ held that she was not a migrant worker, but allowed her claim of inequality of treatment of nationals who exercise their right of freedom of movement on the basis that she was an EU citizen.

In addition, the CJ has had to deal with students who are not 'workers' and thus fall outside Regulation 492/2011. The following cases are illustrative of this issue.

Case	Facts
Gravier v City of Liège	This concerned a French national who applied to study strip cartoon drawing at the Liège Academy des Beaux-Arts in Belgium. She claimed that the imposition of a fee levied on some foreign nationals studying at the Academy was discriminatory and infringed her right of free movement as a recipient of services under Article 56 TFEU.
	The CJ held that where a person fell within the material scope of the Treaties then, by virtue of what is now Article 18 TFEU, they could not be discriminated against on grounds of nationality. Gravier fell within the scope of the Treaty provisions on 'vocational training' previously contained in Article 128 EC (now Article 165 and 166 TFEU).

	The CJ defined 'vocational training' widely as any form of education or training which prepares for a qualification or provides training and skills in relation to a profession, trade or employment, even if that training includes an element of general education. Accordingly, when seeking access to vocational training she could not be treated less favourably than nationals.
	In the present case, the payment of fees higher than those charged to nationals was clearly discriminatory and, therefore, a breach of Article 18 TFEU. This decision was a shock for Member States because it had been assumed that non-workers were entirely beyond the reach of EU law.
Blaizot v University of Liège	The CJ held that even university study can be considered as vocational training for the purposes of what is now Article 18 if it provides education for a qualification or a profession.
	It was pointed out that some university courses are designed to improve general knowledge rather than prepare one for an occupation. Article 18 may not cover these courses of study, although the courses can be vocational if they are followed by a practical stage.
	Thus, the Blaizot ruling covers most university courses and, accordingly, Member States cannot charge higher fees for EU students for those courses.

The CJ has also had to deal with grants for students who are not workers; here is how the law has changed over time:

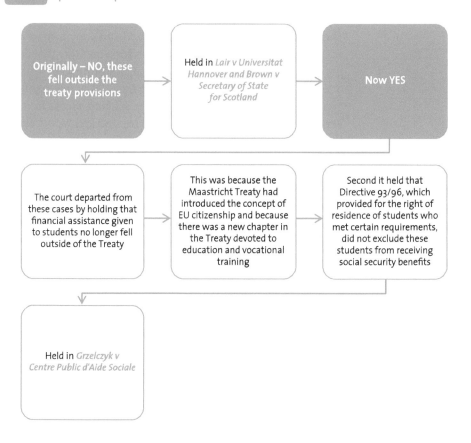

The right of residence for students

Directive 2004/38 does not differentiate between EU citizens if they wish to enter and reside on the territory of one of the Member States for a period of up to three months. However, for those who wish to reside for a period extending beyond the three-month limit, Article 7 of the Directive introduces a simplified system according to which EU citizens are divided into four broad categories:

Article 7 of Directive 2004/38

'(a) a worker or self employed;

(b) a citizen who possesses sufficient resources not to be a burden on social assistance in the host state;

(c) a citizen undergoing a course of study with sufficient resources; and

(d) family members of an EU citizen satisfying the above requirements.'

Category (c) specifically confers a right of residence on individuals who are enrolled at an educational establishment. According to Article 7(1)(c), students can benefit from the right of residence provided they have comprehensive sickness insurance cover and have sufficient financial resources for themselves and their family members so as not to become a burden on the social assistance system of the host State.

Following the rationale of the now repealed Directive 93/96 (Article 3), the new Directive 2004/38 does not give students any right to a maintenance grant.

Grounds for exclusion of workers: Article 45(3) TFEU

Although free movement is one of the key principles, it is still the case that Member States retain some control over exclusion and expulsion of workers. This is contained in Article 45(3) and allows for Member State action on the grounds of public policy, public security and public health. However, these should not be used in a discriminatory, disproportionate or arbitrary way.

To this end, the CJ initially developed and latterly Directive 2004/38 incorporated rules on how Article 45(3) should be used by Member States. The directive contains the following measures:

Key Article	Provides for . . .
Article 27(2)	For the Member State to invoke the public policy derogation, the personal conduct of the individual concerned must represent 'a genuine, present and sufficiently serious threat affecting one of the fundamental interests of society'.
Article 28(1)	Contains safeguards against expulsion, for instance it provides that before deciding to expel an EU citizen on grounds of public policy or public security the Member State's authorities should take account of factors such as how long the individual has resided in the territory of the host State, his/her age, state of health, social and cultural integration and so on.
Article 28(2)	Provides that a Member State must take into account whether a citizen or family member have the right of permanent residence on its territory. If so they can only be expelled on serious grounds of public policy or public security.
Article 28(3)	If they have resided in the host State for at least ten years or are a minor then they may only be expelled on imperative grounds of public security or in the best interests of the child.
Article 29	This deals with public health restrictions. It provides that diseases justifying restrictive measures by Member States must be defined by the relevant instruments of the World Health Organization. Restrictions relating to other contagious diseases are only permissible if they also apply to nationals of the host State. However, diseases occurring after a three-month period from the date of arrival cannot constitute grounds for expulsion.

Note that measures taken on the grounds of public policy and public security must be based 'exclusively on the personal conduct of the individual' whose rights of entry and residence are being challenged and previous criminal convictions are not in themselves sufficient grounds for taking such measures.

As stated the new Directive gives legislative status to principles established by the CJ In the cases of *R v Bouchereau* and *Bonsignore v Oberstadtdirektor der Stadt Köln*.

Key case law and principles

Initial narrow approach

* *Van Duyn v Home Office*
* Van Duyn, a Dutch national, challenged the UK's refusal to allow her entry on the grounds that UK nationals were free to work for Scientology and Scientology's activities were not illegal in the UK. The CJ held that where a Member State has taken administrative measures to restrict the activities of an organisation, that State might rely on the ground of public policy even though it has not made those activities unlawful.

No arbitrary behaviour

* *Adoui and Cornuaille v Belgium State*
* Two French prostitutes were wrongly deported by Belgium because prostitution was not subject to criminal sanctions in Belgium.

Must assess likely future conduct

* *R v Bouchereau*
* This involved a person who had been convicted on two occasions for commercial importation of cocaine on a large scale. A single conviction may be a good ground for deportation in exceptional circumstances, especially if it reveals that the person concerned may be a present danger to society. The CJ said that not only must the person's presence represent such a threat, but that the threat must affect 'one of the fundamental interests of society'.
* Thus, a Member State must show that the person's presence will damage a fundamental interest and not just any aspect of public policy. This will be the case where the individual concerned shows 'a propensity to act in the same way in the future'.

Not as an example to others	*Bonsignore v Oberstadtdirektor der Stadt Köln* ❖ The German authorities ordered the deportation of an Italian worker who had accidentally shot and killed his brother with an unlicensed firearm. The German court had accepted that he had made an error and merely fined him for failing to hold a gun licence. ❖ Nevertheless, the authorities decided to deport him in an attempt to deter others from keeping unlicensed weapons. The CJ ruled that deportation in order to deter others could not be justified The question that must be asked is whether there is a future risk of a breach of public policy or public security that would affect the fundamental interests of society.
Personal conduct	*Criminal proceedings against Donatella Calfa* ❖ The CJ ruled that a Greek law, which required automatic deportation for life for any non national found in possession of drugs for personal use (cannabis in this case), was not compatible with Article 45(3). The blanket rule took no account of the personal conduct of the offender or of the danger that the person posed to the requirements of public policy. ❖ *Astrid Proll v Entry Clearance Officer Dusseldorf* ❖ This involved a member of a 1970s bombing group who subsequently reformed after serving a term in prison. She was invited to work in the UK, but the UK authorities refused her entry. The CJ held that it was possible for individuals to reform and that their propensity to re-offend may therefore be removed despite a notorious past. Entry could not be denied in such cases.

Mutual recognition of professional qualifications

One of the key problems for professionals seeking to move within the EU is non-recognition of qualifications by host Member States. The CJ tackled this in the following case.

> **Case precedent –** *Thieffry v Conseil de l'Ordre des Advocats a la Cour de Paris*

Facts: The French authorities refused to allow the applicant, a Belgian national who had obtained legal qualifications in Belgium which were recognised as adequate to practise in France by a French University, to train at the French bar.

Principle: The CJ found a breach of Articles 49 and 18 TFEU as the conduct amounted to indirect discrimination without justification.

Application: Ensures that workers moving from one state to another are afforded credit for their professional qualifications.

The case law on recognition of professional qualifications has been augmented by Directive 2005/36, which provides for the mutual recognition of professional qualifications. It applies to a number of professions, such as surveying, accountancy and town planning, but not to those covered by specific directives.

It generally involves the recognition by each Member State of certain qualifications achieved after obtaining a higher education diploma on completion of at least three years professional education and the professional training required for that profession.

There are other directives covering other types of education and professions. For example, Directive 98/5 regulates the legal profession.

Putting it into practice

Maria is an Italian citizen who has recently been offered a job in the UK with a large pharmaceutical company.

However, on entry into the UK, she is quizzed heavily over her intentions and asked if she is going to be a burden on the welfare state. In addition, her husband, Carlos, who is Brazilian is told that although he can enter it will only be for one month and he should not attempt either to claim any benefits or find work.

Having finally entered and settled in the UK, Maria is informed at work that she is not eligible for the new company pension scheme as she is not from the UK. She also gets the impression that training opportunities available to her colleagues are not being offered to her because her immediate line manager has doubts about her English language skills.

After two weeks, two further incidents occur. Her ten-year-old son, Lucca, is told that he is not eligible for a school trip which his classmates are going on and her 23-year-old daughter Danielle, who is living with them until she finds work, has been arrested with a small amount of cannabis and threatened with deportation. This is causing her great concern and she has visited you to discuss these issues.

Advise Maria.

Suggested solution

The key is to isolate the issues and deal with each in turn. When there are a number of parties it is also helpful to deal with each party systematically. The key law to start with is Article 45.

Maria

❖ **Introduction**
❖ Has the right to move as an EU worker: Article 45(1), *Lawrie-Blum*.

❖ **Burden on the State**
❖ Maria has the right to be treated without discrimination (Article 45(2)) and has the right to enter the UK to take up work Directive 2004/38.

❖ **Pension**
❖ She has the right to the same social benefits as the UK workers: Regulation 492/2011 Article7(2). Denial of this is direct discrimination: *Commissioner v France*.

❖ **Training**
❖ Again, she has the right to the same opportunities. This would seem to be indirect discrimination. There seems to be no objective justification for not allowing her to take up the training opportunities: *Groener*.

Carlos

❖ **Introduction**
❖ Has the right to move as a spouse of an EU worker: Directive 2004/38 Article 2(2)(a).

❖ **One month**
❖ He can stay as long as the worker although a visa may be required: Directive 2004/38 Articles 4 and 5.

❖ **Benefits**
❖ Social and tax advantages will also apply to him: Regulation 492/2011 Article 7(2) and *Even*.

❖ **Work**
❖ Under Article 23 of Directive 2004/38, he has the right to seek and take up work: *Gul*.

Lucca

❖ **Introduction**
❖ Has the right to move as the descendant of an EU worker under 21: Directive 2004/38 Article 2(2)(c).

❖ **School trip**
❖ He has the right to the same educational opportunities as UK schoolchildren: Regulation 492/2011 Article 10 and *Echternach and Moritz*.

Danielle

❖ **Introduction**
❖ Has the right to move as a dependant of an EU worker: Directive 2004/38 Article 2(2)(c).

❖ **Deportation**
❖ The test is contained in Directive 2004/38 Article 27(2) as developed from *Bouchereau* and *Bonsignore*. It is unlikely that Danielle is 'a genuine, present and sufficiently serious threat' and so the threat of deportation would be disproportionate.

Table of key cases referred to in this chapter

Case name	Area of law	Principle
Adoui and Cornuaille v Belgium State C115 & 116/81 [1982] ECR 1665	Expulsion and exclusion	Expulsion could not be granted as the parties were being treated differently from the MS nationals.
Astrid Proll v Entry Clearance Officer Dusseldorf (1988) 2 CMLR 387	Expulsion and exclusion	It is possible for people to change their behaviour and not be a current threat.
Bettray v Staatsecretaris van Justitie C344/87 [1989] ECR 1621	Definition of worker	Worker in a drug rehab unit fell outside the definition of worker as the treatment was the main objective.
Blaizot v University of Liège C24/86 [1988] ECR 379	Education rights	University study can be considered vocational training.

Bonsignore v Oberstadtdirektor der Stadt Köln C67/74 [1975] ECR 297	Expulsion and exclusion	A key case illustrating the test for expulsion.
Brown v Secretary of State for Scotland C197/86 [1988] ECR 3205	Education rights	Grants are available as they are to national students.
Casagrande v Landeshauptstadt München C9/74 [1974] ECR 773	Education rights	Children of migrant workers are entitled to the same educational opportunities as nationals.
Collins v Secretary of State for Work and Pensions C138/02 [2004] ECR 1–2073	Job seekers	They are not in the same category as workers.
Commission v France (the 'Nurses' case) C307/84 [1986] ECR 1725)	Article 45(4)	Nurses in France did not qualify under this derogation.
Commission v France (French Merchant Seamen) C167/73 [1974] ECR 359	Article 45(4)	French sailors did not qualify under this derogation.
Criminal Proceedings against Donatella Calfa C348/96 ECR I–11	Expulsion and exclusion	This was a disproportionate approach by the state.
Cristini v SNCF C32/75 [1975] ECR 1085	Workers and families rights	A right to a rail reduction was claimed for.
Diatta v Land Berlin C267/83 [1985] ECR 567	Divorce and separation	Separation from an EU spouse does not automatically led to expulsion.

Case name	Area of law	Principle
D'Hoop v Office National de l'Emploi C224/98 [2002] ECR I–6191	Education rights	Enabled benefits as an EU citizen.
Echternach and Moritz v Minister van Onderwijs en Wetenschappen C389 & 390/87 [1989] ECR 723)	Education rights	A very wide interpretation was provided here.
Gravier v City of Liège C293/83 [1985] ECR 593	Education rights	This widened the concept of vocational training.
Grzelczyk v Centre Public d'Aide Sociale C184/99 [2001] ECR I–06193	Education rights	French student could claim rights in Belgium.
Groener v Ministry for Education C379/87 [1989] ECR 3967	Indirect discrimination	None was found here as the language rule was justified.
Gül v Regierungspräsident Düsseldorf C131/85 [1986] ECR 1573	Family rights to work	A Turkish doctor with an EU spouse had the right to work in Germany.
Hoeckx v Centre Public d'Aide Sociale de Kalmthout C249/83 [1985] ECR 973	Workers and families rights	Minimum income allowance is a claimable right.
Hoekstra (née Unger) v Bestuur der Bedrijfsvereniging voor Detailhandel en Ambachten C75/63 [1964] ECR 177	Article 45	Worker has a community meaning.
Jia v Migrationjverket C1/105 [2007]	Families	The definition of a dependant was stated here.

Lair v Universitat Hannover C39/86 [1988] ECR 3161	Education rights	Must show link between previous employment and later studies.
Lawrie-Blum v Land Baden-Wurttemberg C66/85 [1986] ECR 2121	Worker	A three-stage test was created by the court.
Levin v Staatssecretaris van Justitie C53/8 [1982] ECR 1035)	Definition of worker	PT chambermaid judged to be a worker.
Kempf v Staatssecretaris van Justitie C139/85 [1986] ECR 1741	Definition of worker	PT music teacher fell within Article 45.
Maria Martinez Sala v Freistaat Bayern C85/96 [1998] ECR I–2691	Education rights	Right to equal treatment.
Netherlands State v Reed C59/85 [1985] ECR 1283	Families	Spouse was extended to include non-married partner.
O'Flynn v Adjudication Officer C237/94 [1996] ECR I–2617	Workers and families rights	Funeral expenses come under this.
Procurer du Royer C48/75 [1976] ECR 497	Job seekers	Job seekers have limited rights under Article 45.
R v Bouchereau C30/77 [1977] ECR 1999	Expulsion and exclusion	There must be a serious and present threat.
R v Immigration Appeal Tribunal, ex parte Antonissen C292/89 [1991] ECR I–745	Job seekers	A Job seeker can remain if economically active.
R v SOS for the Home Department exp Sandhu [1983] 3 CMLR 553	Divorce and separation	Separation from an EU spouse led to expulsion as the EU worker had left the EU.

Case name	Area of law	Principle
R (Bidar) v London Borough of Ealing C209/03 [2005] ECR I–2119	Education rights	Could rely on Article 18 for support.
Reina v Landeskreditbank Baden-Württemberg C65/81 [1982] ECR 33	Workers and families rights	Entitled to a discretionary childbirth loan.
Steymann v Staatssecretaris van Justitie Justitie C196/87 [1988] ECR 6159	Definition of worker	Odd-job man in a religious community was a worker.
Thieffry v Conseil de l'Ordre des Advocats a la Cour de Paris C71/76 [1977] ECR 765	Mutual recognition	Qualifications obtained in one MS must be recognised in another.
Van Duyn v Home Office (Case 41/74) [1974] ECR 1337	Expulsion and exclusion	An early discredited case on expulsion.
Walrave & Koch v Association Union Cycliste Internationale C36/74 [1974] ECR1405	Definition of worker	Non-competing cyclists were workers.
Württembergische Milchverwertung-Südmilch-AG v Salvatore Ugliola C15/69 [1970] ECR 363	Indirect discrimination	There was no justification for the rule in this case.

@ **Visit the book's companion website to test your knowledge**

❖ Resources include a subject map, revision tip podcasts, downloadable diagrams, MCQ quizzes for each chapter, and a flashcard glossary

❖ www.routledge.com/cw/optimizelawrevision

8

Competition Law I: Article 101 TFEU

Revision objectives

Understand the law

- Have you grasped the basic point of Article 101 and how it works in practice?

Remember the details

- Can you outline the different elements of the Article and show which defence would be applicable?

Reflect critically on areas of debate

- Do you understand the reluctance of the Court of Justice to fully embrace the rule of reason?

Contextualise

- Can you set the law from this chapter alongside the law on free movement of goods and compare and contrast?

Apply your skills and knowledge

- Can you apply this knowledge to a problem-style question?

Chapter Map

Introduction

Previous chapters have identified the problems created by states which are overzealous in protecting their domestic markets. However, it is also the case that individual enterprises or undertakings can also be a hindrance to the free market aims of the EU.

In regard to this, EU competition law has two basic and complementary aims. First (and in common with the competition law of other non-EU countries), it aims to promote a competitive market economy by enhancing the EU's competitive performance in the global market).

Second, EU competition law aims to prevent barriers to the integration of the single, internal market. In this aim, EU competition law differs from that of other non-EU countries.

Over many centuries, European countries have developed successful national market-based economies. With the creation of the single, internal market, the aim is to reproduce, on a Union scale, the conditions that exist in a national market.

If a market works efficiently and effectively, it becomes impossible to maintain artificially high or low prices in different parts of the market because goods will flow freely from the low-priced areas to the high-priced areas and prices will level out. In relation to the EU, subject to transport costs, if the market is working effectively, then the cost of a product should be broadly the same whether the product is, for example, purchased in London, Madrid or Berlin.

Thus, EU law on the free movement of goods and EU competition law are seen as two sides of the same coin, preventing the distortion of the internal market by either the Member States or private enterprise.

This chapter will focus on Article 101 TFEU and the law relating to anti-competitive agreements.

Sources of EU competition law

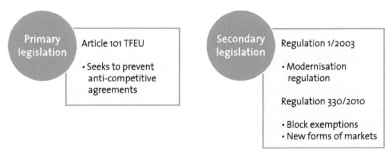

Article 101 TFEU

'1. The following shall be prohibited as incompatible with the internal market: all agreements between undertakings, decisions by associations of undertakings and concerted practices which may affect trade between Member States and which have as their object or effect the prevention, restriction or distortion of competition within the internal market, and in particular those which:
   (a) directly or indirectly fix purchase or selling prices or any other trading conditions;
   (b) limit or control production, markets, technical development, or investment;
   (c) share markets or sources of supply;
   (d) apply dissimilar conditions to equivalent transactions with other trading parties, thereby placing them at a competitive disadvantage; and
   (e) make the conclusion of contracts subject to acceptance by the other parties of supplementary obligations which, by their nature or according to commercial usage, have no connection with the subject of such contracts.
2. Any agreements or decisions prohibited pursuant to this Article shall be automatically void.
3. The provisions of paragraph 1 may, however, be declared inapplicable in the case of:
   (a) any agreement or category of agreements between undertakings;
   (b) any decision or category of decisions by associations of undertakings; and
   (c) any concerted practice or category of concerted practices,
   which contributes to improving the production or distribution of goods or to promoting technical or economic progress, while allowing consumers a fair share of the resulting benefit, and which does not:

   ❖ impose on the undertakings concerned restrictions which are not indispensable to the attainment of these objectives;
   ❖ afford such undertakings the possibility of eliminating competition in respect of a substantial part of the products in question.'

The elements of Article 101

What are 'undertakings'?

The Commission and the EU courts have interpreted 'undertakings' to include any legal or natural person engaged in some form of economic or commercial activity involving the provision of goods or services.

Examples of undertakings include individuals, limited companies (even if based or incorporated outside the EU), partnerships, trade associations, the professions, non-profit-making organisations and state organisations which carry on economic or commercial activities.

Undertakings can include any entity engaged in economic activity regardless of the legal status of the entity and the way in which it is financed (see *Hofner & Else v Macroton GmbH* (Case C-41/90) [1991] ECR I-1979) and can include trade associations. Further examples include:

Name	Decision
Distribution of Package Tours During the 1990 World Cup Decision	FIFA (the body responsible for the 1990 Football World Cup), the Italian football association and the local organising committee were undertakings and were caught by Article 101.
Motosykletistiki Omospondia Ellados NPID (MOTOE) v Elliniko Domosio	ELPA was a non-profit-making, legal body having sole public power to grant the authorisation of motorcycle events in Greece. It did, however, also organise such events for itself from which it gained money from sponsorship, advertising and insurance contracts. ELPA refused to grant authorisation of a rival organisation's event and the CJ stated that ELPA amounted to an undertaking because it was engaged in an economic activity and this was irrespective of ELPA's legal form and the way it was financed.
	The fact that it was non profit-making was also irrelevant as it still competed with other operators which did seek to make a profit. In such a context its public powers gave it such an obvious advantage over them that the refusal of authorisation amounted to abuse.
Transocean Marine Paint Association v Commission	Recommendations relating to market strategies came from the trade association which was deemed to fall within the definition of an 'undertaking'.
ANSEAU/NAVEWA	A trade association was involved with the supply of washing machines and dishwashers.
	The trade association provided that such goods could only be distributed under a common label and this was held to amount to a decision under Article 101(1).

By examining the above cases you can see that the CJEU takes a very broad approach to the definition of an undertaking which should be borne in mind when considering the parties in a problem-style question.

The structure of the Article

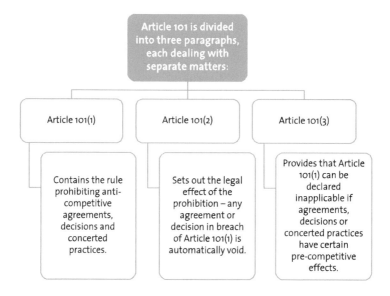

Article 101(1) EC

Article 101(1) contains three elements, each of which needs to be satisfied before the prohibition takes effect.

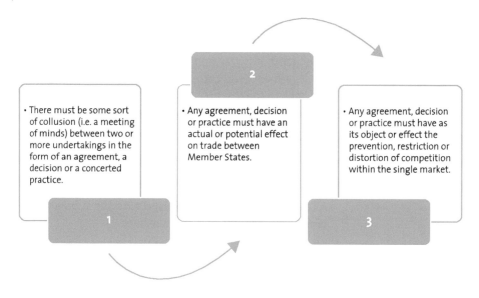

Case precedent – *AC Treuhand AG v Commission*

Facts: A consultancy firm contributed actively and intentionally to a cartel between organic peroxide producers by storing secret documents, collecting and distributing commercial information amongst the members, organising meetings and reimbursing expenses so as to conceal the cartel.

Principle: The firm was guilty of collusion even though not a party to the agreement itself nor was it operating in the same market as the cartel. It was enough that the claimant actively contributed and that there was a sufficiently definite and decisive causal link between the activity and the restriction of competition on the peroxide market.

Application: This illustrates the width of the approach employed indicating a robust approach to competition law.

Agreements, decisions and concerted practices

Article 101(1) identifies three forms of collusion, which breach the article when they prevent, restrict or distort competition. They are: agreements between undertakings; decisions by associations of undertakings; and concerted practices.

Collusion might involve a formal contract or an informal agreement or arrangement. The important distinction is between non-collusive (or independent) behaviour, which is lawful, and collusive behaviour, which is unlawful.

Agreements between undertakings
This has been widely interpreted and applied by the court:

> **It can mean both oral and written agreements**
>
> • *Tepea v Commission*

> **And so-called 'gentlemen's agreements'**
>
> • *Hercules Chemicals NV v Commission*

> **But not unilateral behaviour**
>
> • *Bayer AG v Commission*

Concerted practices

The term 'concerted practice' in Article 101(1) is intended to catch those forms of co-operation that do not amount to a formal oral or written agreement, or a decision.

A concerted practice may be any co-ordinated or parallel behaviour where there is little evidence of an agreement, other than the suspicious behaviour itself. The behaviour may be strong evidence of a concerted practice where it leads to market conditions that do not appear to be normal and competitive. For example, it might be the case that, over a short period of time, a number of energy companies announce price increases: is this a genuine move caused by market forces such as a scarcity of raw materials, or, is it simply because they can?

The 'Dyestuffs' case

Here the CJ defined a 'concerted practice' as:

> ' . . . a form of coordination between undertakings which, without having reached the stage where an agreement properly so-called has been concluded, knowingly substitutes practical cooperation between them for the risks of competition.'

Case precedent – *ICI v Commission* (the 'Dyestuffs' case)

Facts: A subsidiary of ICI within the EU increased the price of a bleaching agent. The remainder of the competitors in the same market then increased their respective prices within a short space of time and by the same margin.
Similar price increases occurred on three separate occasions.

ICI attempted to justify its actions on the basis that it was operating in an oligopolistic market and, because the market had so few competitors, so called 'parallel pricing' was inevitable.

Principle: It was decided that the competitors had been guilty of price fixing through concerted practices and fined them.

There was a high degree of coordination between the producers who had raised their prices by similar amounts on three different occasions.

The rates of individual price increases were the same in all the relevant countries and, generally, related to the same products. The price increases were put into effect on almost the same day.

The orders put out by a number of the producers contained very similar wording and were sent out on the same day. The court also had evidence that producers attended meetings in Basel and London.

Application: This illustrates the possible width of interpretation of what constitutes an agreement under Article 101.

The term 'trade' in Article 101 TFEU has been given a wide meaning. It includes the production and distribution of goods, including agricultural produce, and the services sector, including areas such as banking, insurance and maritime transport.

The agreement or behaviour must have direct effect on trade in the EU. The following cases are good examples of the court's approach to effect on trade:

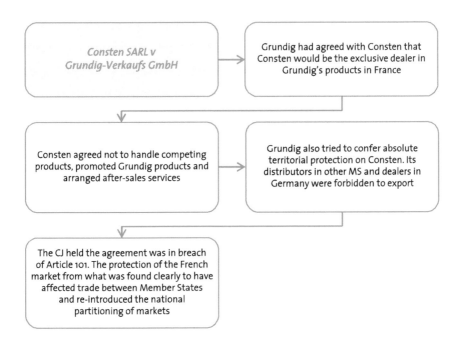

Consten SARL v Grundig-Verkaufs GmbH → Grundig had agreed with Consten that Consten would be the exclusive dealer in Grundig's products in France

Consten agreed not to handle competing products, promoted Grundig products and arranged after-sales services → Grundig also tried to confer absolute territorial protection on Consten. Its distributors in other MS and dealers in Germany were forbidden to export

The CJ held the agreement was in breach of Article 101. The protection of the French market from what was found clearly to have affected trade between Member States and re-introduced the national partitioning of markets

---

Case precedent – *Brasserie de Haecht SA v Wilkin-Janssen*

Facts: The relevant agreement was between a Belgian brewery and a small number of pubs operating only in Belgium. The agreement provided that the pubs were to obtain supplies from the brewery exclusively. In defence, it was argued that this was a minor agreement and there was no cross-border trade involved.

Principle: The Commission stated that the agreement might affect trade between Member States even though the agreement concerned Belgium only because the cumulative effect of a number of such agreements would close the Belgian market to foreign importers.

Application: Even the effect of a number of small agreements, if taken collectively, has been found to affect the single market.

The object or effect of prevention, restriction or distortion of competition within the common market

Article 101(1) applies to all agreements, whether they are horizontal agreements or vertical agreements:

Horizontal

• Horizontal agreements are agreements between undertakings at the same level of trade or industry, for example, between two or more manufacturers, or two or more wholesalers of goods who compete with each other.

Vertical

• Vertical agreements are agreements between undertakings at different levels of trade or industry, for example, those between a producer and a distributor or wholesaler.

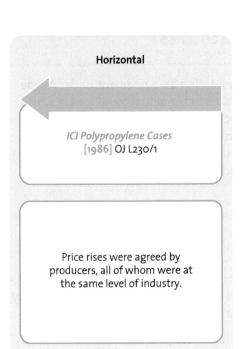

Horizontal

ICI Polypropylene Cases
[1986] OJ L230/1

Price rises were agreed by producers, all of whom were at the same level of industry.

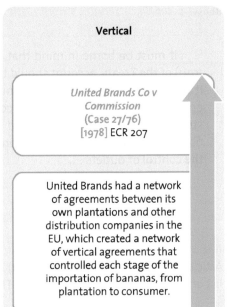

Vertical

United Brands Co v Commission
(Case 27/76)
[1978] ECR 207

United Brands had a network of agreements between its own plantations and other distribution companies in the EU, which created a network of vertical agreements that controlled each stage of the importation of bananas, from plantation to consumer.

Meaning of 'object' and 'effect'

In Article 101(1) TFEU, it is clear that the terms 'object' and 'effect' are regarded as alternative and not cumulative requirements for finding an infringement of Article 101(1).

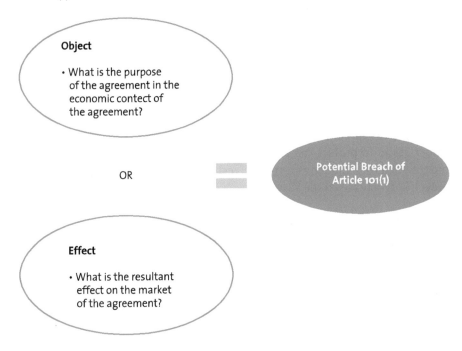

Object

• What is the purpose of the agreement in the economic contect of the agreement?

OR

Potential Breach of Article 101(1)

Effect

• What is the resultant effect on the market of the agreement?

In *European Night Services v Commission*, the CFI stated:

> ' . . . it must be borne in mind that in assessing an agreement under Article 101(1) of the Treaty, account should be taken of the actual conditions in which it functions, in particular the economic context in which the undertakings operate, the products or services covered by the agreement and the actual structure of the market concerned . . . unless it is an agreement containing obvious restrictions of competition such as price-fixing, market-sharing or the control of outlets . . . '

Meaning of preventing, restricting or distorting competition

Article 101(1) sets out in paragraphs (a) to (e) a non-exhaustive (or illustrative only) list of restrictions that are prohibited. These include:

- ❖ directly or indirectly fix purchase or selling prices (ie price-fixing);
- ❖ the fixing of any trading conditions;
- ❖ effectively, this prohibits export bans and bans on parallel imports;
- ❖ limit or control production, markets, technical development or investment; and
- ❖ apply dissimilar conditions to equivalent transactions with other trading parties, thereby placing them at a competitive disadvantage.

Defences to Article 101(1)

One difficulty that the Commission or a National Competition Agency often faces is that an agreement may contain some elements restricting competition as well as some pro-competitive elements.

For example, an agreement may allow the sale of a product for the first time in a Member State. To protect the distributor, the agreement may contain some anti-competitive elements, such as territorial restrictions. It may also be pro-competitive, however, if it increases trade.

Overall, it may have a beneficial economic impact and the Commission or an NCA may allow the agreement to stand if it falls within the ambit of Article 101(3). Three key defences have emerged:

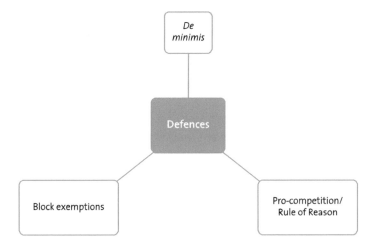

De minimis

An agreement that falls within the terms of Article 101(1) may nevertheless not be caught because it does not have an appreciable effect on, either, competition or inter-state trade.

Case precedent – *Völk v Vervaecke*

Facts: A German producer of washing machines had granted an exclusive distributorship to Vervaecke in Belgium and Luxembourg and guaranteed it absolute territorial protection against parallel imports. Völk's share in the washing machine market was negligible (0.2% of German production and 0.08% of EU production).

Principle: The Court held that an agreement falls outside the prohibition in Article 85 (now Article 101) when it has only an insignificant effect on the markets, taking into account the weak position which the persons concerned have on the market of the product in question.

Application: This defence applies to agreements the object or effect of which is to prevent competition, and to both horizontal and vertical agreements. To establish whether an agreement has an insignificant effect, the Commission or NCA (subject to review by the courts) must determine the market share and what is the relevant market.

This has been formalised by the Notice on Agreements of Minor Importance 2001. Market share under the following limits is regarded as *de minimis* and does not have an appreciable effect on the market.

Horizontal agreements	Vertical agreements
An aggregate share not exceeding 10%	An aggregate share not exceeding 15%

Notices issued by the Commission are not legally binding and are known as 'soft law'. They are meant as guidelines only.

An agreement, therefore, may be held to be caught by Article 101(1) even though the relevant market share is below the figures set out in the Notice.

Similarly, an agreement may be found not to have an appreciable effect on competition even though the relevant market share is above the figures set out in the Notice.

De minimis is applicable to all anti-competitive agreements and normally means that such an agreement, while technically breaching Article 101(1), is unlikely to be pursued by the Commission.

Summary

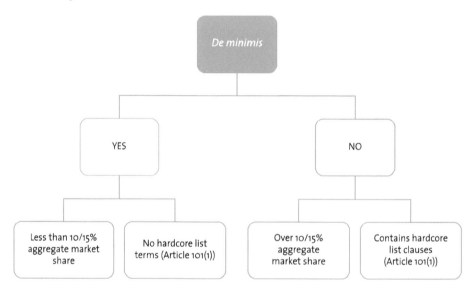

Pro-competition/Rule of reason

If an agreement had both anti-competitive and pro-competitive elements and so technically infringed Article 101(1), the EU courts could determine that the agreement did not, in fact, infringe Article 101(1), if they considered that the pro-competitive elements in the agreement outweighed the anti-competitive ones.

The concept of the rule of reason originally developed in the US because, under American anti-trust laws, there was no power equivalent to the original Article 101(3) by which exemptions might be granted. In the US, the courts decided whether an arrangement breached anti-trust laws by looking at the reason or purpose for the law. If, on balance, an arrangement promoted competition, it would be allowed to operate, even though it technically infringed anti-trust law. This approach has been followed in some notable cases.

Case precedent – *Pronuptia de Paris GmbH v Pronuptia de Paris Irmgard Schillgallis*

Facts: This case involved a dispute in relation to a franchise agreement. Mrs Schillgalis had a franchise from Pronuptia to sell that company's goods (wedding dresses) and related services in her shop.

Generally, a franchise agreement obliges the franchisor (here, Pronuptia) to supply goods, together with knowhow and training and otherwise to support the franchisee (Mrs Schillgalis).

Principle: The Court recognised franchising as a business method that promoted competition – it helps create small businesses and increases consumer choice.

Unless certain anti-competitive clauses were included in the contract (e.g. clauses prohibiting the franchisee from competing with the franchise network and keeping information provided by the franchisor confidential) the franchisor would not be willing to enter into such an agreement.

Application: Both cases illustrate the importance of a flexible, arguably rule of reason approach in order to ensure the existence of good competitive markets.

Case precedent – *Société Technique Minière v Maschinenbau Ulm GmbH* (the 'STM' case)

Facts: This concerned a contract granting exclusive rights to sell heavy machinery in France.

Principle: The court held that a term in a contract conferring exclusivity on a distributor might not infringe Article 101(1) where this seemed to be 'really necessary for the penetration of a new area by an undertaking'.

Application: The court recognised the heavy expenditure and high risk necessary for the company to break into a new market and to sell its machines in France.

If the contract had been found to infringe Article 101(1), presumably the machinery would not have been available for sale in France. The pro-competitive elements in the contract (the development of a new market) were found to outweigh any anti-competitive elements.

However, the existence of such a rule has not been absolutely confirmed by the Community courts. On the contrary, in various judgments the Court of Justice and the Court of First Instance have been at pains to indicate that the existence of a rule of reason in Community law is doubtful despite the use of such an approach above. Block exemptions will be covered later in this chapter.

Article 101(2) has the effect of rendering anti-competitive agreements void, but as noted there is a defence in the form of Article 101(3). In order to satisfy Article 101(3), an agreement must:

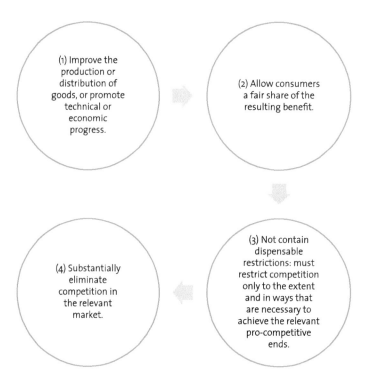

In effect, Article 101(3) recognises that some anti-competitive agreements may provide economic advantages to the single market. For example, where an undertaking is trying to break into (i.e. sell its goods in) a new market, the only commercially effective way to do so may be to enter into an agreement with an undertaking already trading in that market. Introducing a new product into a market will involve considerable expense for both the manufacturer (or producer) and the distributor. It will also involve the risk that the product will not sell.

To make the risk worthwhile, the producer may enter into an agreement granting the distributor the sole rights to sell the product in the relevant market. While such an agreement is anti-competitive (because it prevents other traders from selling the product), the agreement may still result in an overall increase in trade and the new product being available to more consumers in more Member States.

Case precedent – *Transocean Marine Paint Association v Commission*

Facts: An agreement was entered into between members of the Transocean Marine Paint Association. The agreement provided the respective parties with some (although not absolute) territorial protection.

Principle: The Commission recognised the overall benefit to the single market that the agreement provided (in distributing marine paint) and granted an exemption even though the agreement divided the market into national blocks.

Application: This allowed the creating and consolidating of markets for a niche product.

Thus, the agreement may have a positive effect on the single market and the Commission or an NCA may view the agreement favourably. As long as the agreement complies with the conditions in Article 101(3) or falls within the categories of block exemptions created by the Commission under Article 101(3), it will be allowed to operate.

It is clear that Article 101(1) and (3) TFEU and Regulation 1/2003 work together. Under Regulation 1/2003, an undertaking (with legal advice) may decide whether what it is doing is caught by Article 101(1) or falls within the ambit of Article 101(3).

If that decision is challenged; by a competitor, by the Commission or the NCAs on their own initiative, the Commission or the NCAs will determine if the requirements of Article 101 are met.

Decisions of the Commission are subject to review by the EU courts. Decisions of an NCA are subject to review by the national court of the relevant NCA.

Aim Higher

Do you understand why the EU allows for a mechanism to balance between pro and anti-competitive effects?

Can you think of illustrations demonstrating the robust approach towards breaches of competition law employed by the EU authorities? The case law in this chapter will help to substantiate your answer.

Summary

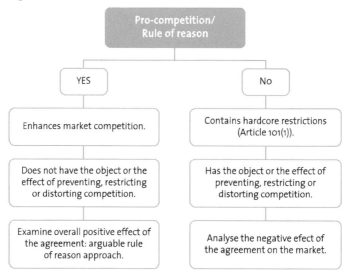

Block exemptions and Regulation 1/2003

The Commission from time to time issues 'block exemptions', the effect of which is to exempt a whole category of agreements from the operation of Article 101(1). As long as the conditions set out in Article 101(3) are fulfilled, undertakings do not have to notify the Commission of their intention to enter into agreements that potentially might infringe Article 101(1) but come within a block exemption. Such agreements are valid without authorisation.

Thus, there are two main benefits of the block exemption system: First, it provides legal certainty for undertakings; second, it has relieved the Commission of a considerable amount of work.

The operation of Regulation 1/2003 does not affect the granting of block exemptions – only the Commission can grant them. However, both the Commission and the NCAs may, under Article 29 of Regulation 1/2003, determine whether an agreement is within the terms of a block exemption.

Each block exemption will also confer on the Commission (and sometimes the NCAs) the power to withdraw the benefit of a block exemption if an agreement has a detrimental effect on competition.

Regulation 330/2010 and block exemptions

Regulation 330/2010 is an example of a block exemption. It block exempts certain vertical agreements between undertakings at different levels of the production or distribution chain. The key component articles are outlined in the following table:

Article 1	Definitions of terminology used
Article 2	Provides the exemption granted to Vertical Agreements under the provisions of A101(3).
Article 3	Provides the market share threshold or *de minimis* requirements.
Article 4	Provides the hardcore restrictions.
Article 5	Provides the non-compete restrictions.
Article 6	Provides for non-application of the Regulation.
Article 7	Deals with the manner of application of Article 3 (e.g. if agreements stray over the 30% threshold).

In addition, a more detailed analysis of the Regulation shows that for an undertaking to satisfy the block exemption rules, there are a number of criteria to be satisfied:

Article 2(1)
- ❖ Contains the main provision of the block exemption and sets out the vertical agreements to which the exemption applies.

Article 3(1)
- ❖ Provides that undertakings with a market share of more than 30% will not qualify for block exemption.

  Note that in a vertical agreement both the supplier's and the buyer's market shares must fall below 30% (individual shares not cumulative).

Article 4
- ❖ Contains the hardcore provisions which an agreement must not contain if it is to qualify for the block exemption. Where an undertaking can demonstrate that an infringement has got either: objective justification, or market efficiency then the Commission may allow this as a justification in individual cases.

Hardcore provisions
- ❖ (1) Price-fixing – no minimum price is permitted, although maximum and non-enforceable recommended prices are acceptable, and there must be no restriction on the buyer's ability to set its own prices.
- ❖ (2) Territorial restrictions – restrictions on active selling (actively approaching customers) are acceptable, but an agreement must not stop passive selling (responding to unsolicited requests from customers), of which websites are an example.

Article 5

> ❖ Prohibits certain other terms that are not considered hardcore. An agreement may still gain the benefit of block exemption if the offending terms can be severed or struck out and the agreement makes sense legally and linguistically without those terms (e.g. a non-compete obligation) (where one party to an agreement agrees not to compete with the other party for a certain period). If non-compete clauses are indefinite or last over five years, they are prohibited.

Articles 6–7

> ❖ A block exemption may be withdrawn if the vertical agreement (either individually or jointly with others) falls within Article 101(1) and fails to succeed under Article 101(3) or does so in a territory of a Member State. Effectively the block exemption is incompatible with Article 101.

Summary

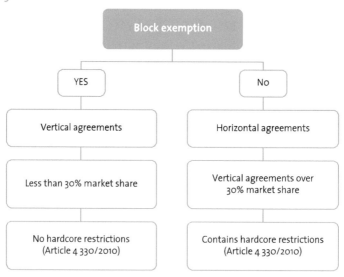

Regulation 330/2010 and the internet

The advent of internet retailing has provided the EU with further areas which need regulation. With regard to internet sales, the Commission has sought to balance the obvious advantage of the internet to the EU in maximising inter-state trade with providing protection to those distributors' investing in 'bricks and mortar' and marketing, etc.

Restrictions on internet selling by distributors will generally be considered a hardcore offence. Once a supplier has allowed a distributor into its distribution agreement it cannot stop the distributor selling online. The Commission considers that consumers should not face obstacles because of the Member State in which they live.

However, there is flexibility in the Commission's approach. Within the context of internet selling the concept of active and passive selling remains the same but has been refined from the benefit of past experience. A simple website remains passive selling (as long as it is not targeted at a territory from which the distributor is excluded by the vertical agreement) while the inclusion of language options on such a site is still passive selling.

However, sending unsolicited e-mails to customers or to particular territorial areas is active selling, as are online adverts specifically addressed to customers outside the distributor's territory. The latter could include banner adverts on a third-party website (adverts which pop up or appear scrolled ('bannered') across the top of such a website when consumers access them about related matters (or even unrelated)).

So within this context selective and exclusive distribution agreements (where distributors are selected on the basis of specified criteria and only allowed to sell within a specified territory) will be allowed to restrict active selling but passive selling restrictions are still hardcore (Article 1(1)(e)).

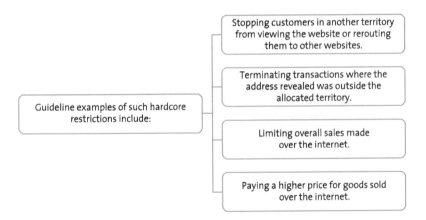

Guideline examples of such hardcore restrictions include:

- Stopping customers in another territory from viewing the website or rerouting them to other websites.
- Terminating transactions where the address revealed was outside the allocated territory.
- Limiting overall sales made over the internet.
- Paying a higher price for goods sold over the internet.

Enforcement of Article 101 TFEU by the Commission and the NCAs under Regulation 1/2003

Regulation 1/2003 has brought about fundamental changes in the way that EU competition law is enforced. The principal change is that it devolves authority from the Commission to NCAs. The monopolistic powers originally granted only to the Commission are now shared throughout the ECN.

The system of obtaining individual exemptions from the Commission is abolished, as is the use of comfort letters, in this context. Now, the parties to an agreement, decision or concerted practice must themselves (with legal advice) decide if an agreement infringes Articles 101 and/or 102.

The power to apply Articles 101 and 102 is in the hands of the Commission and the NCAs.

The national courts of Member States may also apply Articles 101 and 102 directly and will deal with appeals from decisions of the NCAs. These courts may become involved when a competitor, an NCA, or the Commission, on their own initiative, challenge the decision of the parties that an agreement does not infringe Article 101.

Infringement of Article 101 has serious consequences for guilty undertakings. The current sanction for a breach of this Article is contained in Article 23 of the Regulation and is a fine of up to 10% of worldwide turnover in the preceding year.

Putting it into practice

Goethe SA is a German company specialising in the manufacturing of washing machines and dishwashers. They have concentrated on the German market for a number of years but have been approached by a Belgian retail chain, Mercier, who wish to stock and sell their products. Mercier estimate that they can capture 25% of the relevant product market within 18 months to two years. In order to facilitate this, a draft contract has been submitted to Goethe from the law firm representing Mercier. As an in-house lawyer for Goethe, you have been asked by the chief executive to assess the legality of the terms in this document.
The proposed contract reads as follows;

Term 1: Mercier will act as exclusive vendors for Goethe in Belgium.

Term 2: Minimum prices are to be fixed by Mercier.

Term 3: Goethe are not allowed to advertise or market their products in Belgium.

Term 4: Mercier can also sell through some of their branches which they have recently opened in France and Goethe cannot sell to other French retailers.

Term 5: Belgian customers atttempting to use the Goethe website must be rerouted to Mercier's website.

Suggested solution

In such a question, it is advisable to set up the area using the key law then go through and assess each term in turn.

Introduction

You should state that this is governed by Article 101 TFEU and outline the key elements of the law. Also that Regulation 1/2003 has placed the burden on the companies themselves to self-assess the legality of their behaviour. This is a vertical exclusive distribution agreement between undertakings and as such could engage Article 101.

Possible defences:

❖ de minimis (Volk/NAOMI) – only available if less than 15% combined market share – Mercier envisage a greater percentage
❖ Articles 101 and 103 Rule of reason (*STM*) – they are breaking into a new market
❖ Block exemptions under Regulation 330/2010 – each term will be assessed.

Term 1

This term is probably OK as this is a common way for companies to share risk and move into different territories. The case of *Consten v Grundig* is illustrative.

Term 2

This term is a hardcore restriction and is not permitted under *de minimis*, is outlawed by Article 101(1)(a) and is not allowed under Regulation 330/2010 Article 4: *United Brands*.

Term 3

This term is an example of a restriction on active selling which can be allowed. Active selling is where an undertaking is prevented from actively pursuing customers as opposed to a restriction on passive selling where you cannot refuse to deal with a customer who approaches you: *Calor Gas*.

Term 4

This is an example of a non-compete term whereby undertakings agree not to compete with each other in different territories. This can be allowed under the Regulation but not if exceeding a five-year period. They are also allowed under the rule of reason as long as the conditions are not too prohibitive: *Transocean Marine Paint*.

Term 5

This is an example of a recent innovation in the law to deal with the growth of internet retail. Regulation 330/2010 contains restrictions which would apply here. This is an example of a restriction on passive selling which would be prohibited.

Conclusion

Overall, your advice should be that this contract is not acceptable. The *de minimis* defence may not be available and overall this restricts rather than enhances competition. Terms 2 & 5 should be struck out and Term 4 needs to be clarified. If the contract is entered into between the parties, the NCA can investigate and ultimately fine under Regulation 1/2003.

Table of key cases referred to in this chapter

Case name	Area of law	Principle
AC Treuhand AG v Commission CT99/04 [2008] WLR (D) 229	Article 101(1)	This demonstrates the broad approach adopted to 101.
ANSEAU/NAVEWA [1982] 2 CMLR 193	Undertakings	Trade associations can be undertakings.
Bayer AG v Commission T41/96 [2000] ECR II-3383	Agreements	Unilateral behaviour falls outside agreement.
Brasserie de Haecht SA v Wilkin-Janssen C3/67 [1967] ECR 407	Effect on trade	Even if all the agreements are in one state, this can still have a negative effect on trade in the EU.
Consten SARL v Grundig-Verkaufs GmbH C56 and 58/64 [1966] ECR 299	Effect on trade	Vertical distribution agreements can have a negative effect on competition.
Distribution of Package Tours During the 1990 World Cup Decision C92/521 [1992] OJ L 326/31	Undertakings	The organising body was deemed to fall within Article 101.
European Night Services v Commission T-374, 375, 384, 388/94 [1998] ECR II-3141	Object and effect	This case has an illuminating statement on the meaning of these words.
Hercules Chemicals NV v Commission T-7/89 [1991] ECR II-1711	Agreements	Gentleman's agreements are included.
ICI v Commission (the 'Dyestuffs' case) C48/69 [1972] ECR 619	Collusion	The behaviour of cartels can lead to allegations of collusion.

ICI Polypropylene Cases [1986] OJ L230/1	Vertical v Horizontal	An example of a horizontal cartel market.
Motosykletistiki Omospondia Ellados NPID (MOTOE) v Elliniko Domosio C49/07) [2009] All ER (EC) 150	Undertakings	Sports bodies can be undertakings.
Pronuptia de Paris GmbH v Pronuptia de Paris Irmgard Schillgallis C161/84 [1986] ECR 353	Rule of reason	To encourage trade, certain terms may be interpreted more favourably than usual.
Société Technique Minière v Maschinenbau Ulm GmbH (the '*STM*' case) C56/65 [1966] ECR 235)	Rule of reason	Breaking into a new market is a good reason for a light touch approach by the authorities.
Transocean Marine Paint Association v Commission C17/74 [1974] ECR 1063)	Undertakings	Trade associations can be undertakings.
Tepea v Commission [1978] 3 CMLR 392	Agreements	Oral and written can be included.
United Brands Co v Commission C27/76 [1978] ECR 207	Vertical v Horizontal	An example of a vertical supply chain agreement.
Völk v Vervaecke C5/69 [1969] ECR 295	*De minimis*	This case introduced this defence.

@ Visit the book's companion website to test your knowledge

❖ Resources include a subject map, revision tip podcasts, downloadable diagrams, MCQ quizzes for each chapter, and a flashcard glossary

❖ www.routledge.com/cw/optimizelawrevision

9

Competition Law II: Article 102 TFEU

Revision objectives

Understand the law	• Have you grasped the basic point of Article 102 and how it works in practice?
Remember the details	• Can you outline the different elements of the Article and show which markets would be applicable?
Reflect critically on areas of debate	• Do you understand the approach of the Court of Justice in determining dominance?
Contextualise	• Can you set the law from this chapter alongside the law on free movement of workers and compare and contrast?
Apply your skills and knowledge	• Can you apply this knowledge to a problem-style question?

Chapter Map

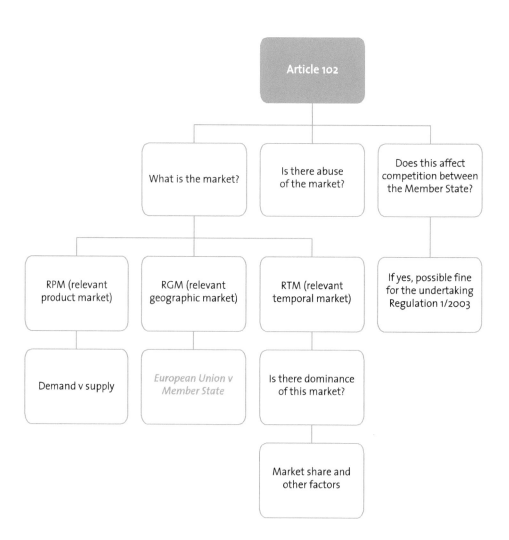

Introduction

This chapter examines Article 102 TFEU. Article 102 seeks to deal with the threat to competition within the market posed by an undertaking which enjoys a dominant position and has the economic power to act independently of the market.

However, Article 102 does not prohibit market dominance in itself. Indeed, dominance in a market can indicate that an undertaking is operating more efficiently than its rivals, and efficiency is one of the aims of competition law. Instead, Article 102 prohibits the abuse of a dominant position that is capable of affecting trade between Member States. Abuse includes anti-competitive behaviour which eliminates or seriously weakens competition in a market (e.g. by using a dominant position to weaken or drive smaller competitors out of the market) or which prevents potential competitors from entering the market or enables a dominant undertaking to exploit its customers. All these types of conduct lead to a distortion of competition.

Sources of EU competition law

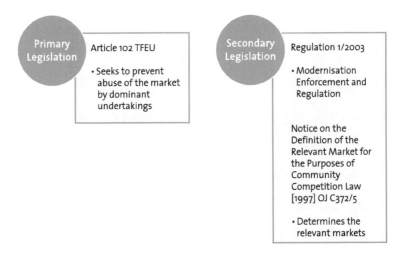

Article 102 TFEU

Article 102 states:

'Any abuse by one or more undertakings of a dominant position within the internal market or in a substantial part of it shall be prohibited as incompatible with the internal market in so far as it may affect trade between Member States.
    Such abuse may, in particular, consist in:

    (a) directly or indirectly imposing unfair purchase or selling prices or other unfair trading conditions;

(b) limiting production, markets or technical development to the prejudice of consumers;

(c) applying dissimilar conditions to equivalent transactions with other trading parties, thereby placing them at a competitive disadvantage;

(d) making the conclusion of contracts subject to acceptance by the other parties of supplementary obligations which, by their nature or according to commercial usage, have no connection with the subject of such contracts.'

In order to determine whether Article 102 is engaged, the Commission and the NCA's will have regard to the following questions:

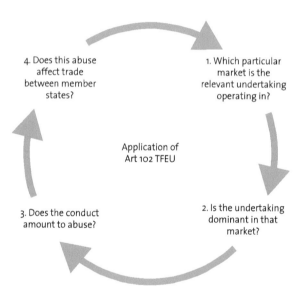

4. Does this abuse affect trade between member states?

1. Which particular market is the relevant undertaking operating in?

Application of Art 102 TFEU

3. Does the conduct amount to abuse?

2. Is the undertaking dominant in that market?

What is the market?

In order to show that the behaviour of a dominant undertaking has offended against Article 102, it is necessary for the Commission (or an NCA) to determine in precisely what 'market' that undertaking is operating.

The concept of a market is an economic one and defining the 'market' for particular goods or services can be a highly complex exercise requiring sophisticated economic analysis by expert witnesses.

The Notice on the Definition of the Relevant Market for the Purposes of Community Competition Law [1997] OJ C372/5, the Commission has provided some guidance is determining the market. In particular, in paragraph 2, it states:

Market definition is a tool to identify and define the boundaries of competition between firms. It serves to establish the framework within which competition policy is applied by the Commission. The main purpose of market definition is to identify in a systematic way the competitive constraints that the undertakings involved face. The objective of defining a market in both its product and geographic dimension is to identify those actual competitors of the undertakings involved that are capable of constraining those undertakings' behaviour and of preventing them from behaving independently of effective competitive pressure.

Thus, there are three relevant concepts to determining the 'market', namely:

| Relevant Product Market (RPM) | Relevant Geographic Market (RGM) | Relevant Temporal Market (RTM) |

The Relevant Product Market (RPM)

Establishing the RPM will often involve detailed, expensive and sometimes controversial market analysis by experts, including both economists and lawyers. Because of the complexity of market analysis, investigations by the Commission or an NCA can take a long time. Even after a long and detailed investigation, the definition by the Commission or NCA of a particular market can be highly contentious.

> **Case precedent – *Hilti AG v Commission* (Case T-30/89A) [1990] ECR II-163 and (Case C-53/92P) [1994] ECR I-667**
>
> **Facts:** Hilti produced nail guns. They went to a great deal of expense commissioning their own report in an attempt to show that the RPM for nail guns was not simply 'nail guns' in themselves but rather the general market of industrial fasteners, of which nail guns were merely a small part. They argued that the RPM included other means of fastening, such as masonry drills. If this broader RPM was accepted, Hilti's place in the overall market was relatively small and they could not offend Article 102 as they could not be dominant.
>
> **Principle:** This argument was not accepted by the Commission or the CJ, which found that nail guns were sufficiently unique as a product to occupy a

separate part of the industrial fasteners market (i.e. a sub-market). In this smaller submarket, Hilti held a dominant position.

Application: It is possible for markets to be sub-divided into smaller micro markets in which undertakings are then dominant.

In addition, Hilti had a market share of 70–80% which was clearly regarded as a dominant position.

Product substitution – Interchangeability of the product

One of the key approaches adopted by the Commission and the court is to ask whether the consumer would regard a product as substitutable or interchangeable. In practice, this means ascertaining whether the customer would accept a substitute product if their original choice was not available. For example, if you went to the store to buy an iPad and the particular model you wanted was unavailable – how likely is it that you would buy a substitute product, perhaps from another, rival manufacturer such as Samsung?

If the answer is yes, 'I would choose another product' then the product is substitutable and the market has many potential competitors. If the answer is negative, then it may be posited that the product is unique and non-substitutable, perhaps dominating this particular RPM.

Where one item is readily interchangeable with another it is unlikely that the producer of one of the items will have a dominant position. If that producer were to raise his or her prices, or reduce quality or quantity, consumers would simply buy the rival's substitute product. The extent to which products can be regarded as substitutes for one another involves an analysis of what economists describe as the cross-elasticity of supply and demand.

Hilti is one example. One of the most notable is below.

Case precedent – *United Brands Company and United Brands Continentaal BV v Commission of the European Communities* (Chiquita Bananas)

Facts: The issue arose as to whether bananas were part of the overall fruit market or whether bananas formed a separate market of their own. If the former was the case, then United Brands would not be dominant in the market as they only had a small share of the fruit market. If, however, the latter was the case, then United Brands would be dominant. In deciding the case, the CJ looked at whether the banana had any peculiar or distinct features which distinguished it from other fruit, so that it was not interchangeable with other fruit

Principle: The CJ found that the banana was soft and seedless and so it could be eaten by the very young and the very old or the sick. Such consumers were unlikely to be able to buy other fruits as substitutes. As a consequence, the banana was in constant demand and sales were unaffected by seasonal fluctuations.

Application: The CJ considered, on the basis of these facts that the banana was in a specialised, sub-market of its own, separate from the overall fruit market. Consumers were not able readily to find substitutes for the banana – there was low cross-elasticity of demand.

Although United Brands had a market a share of only around 40–45%, they were regarded as dominant as the rest of the market was fragmented with their nearest rival only having 17% of the market.

Substitutability: Demand v supply
Interchangeability, product substitution, or cross-elasticity may occur at either the supply or demand sides of the market.

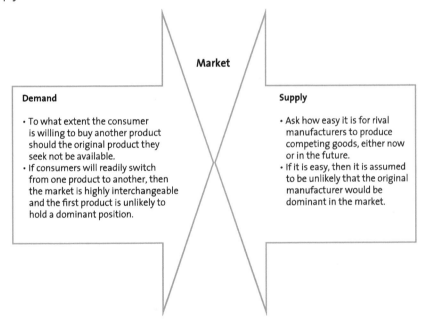

Market

Demand

- To what extent the consumer is willing to buy another product should the original product they seek not be available.
- If consumers will readily switch from one product to another, then the market is highly interchangeable and the first product is unlikely to hold a dominant position.

Supply

- Ask how easy it is for rival manufacturers to produce competing goods, either now or in the future.
- If it is easy, then it is assumed to be unlikely that the original manufacturer would be dominant in the market.

SSNIP test
To assist with determining cross-elasticity, the Notice on the Definition of the Relevant Market sets out a test for demand substitution. The test originated in the United States of America and is called the SSNIP test. It looks at the effect of a Small but Significant (between 5–10%) Non-transitory (i.e. permanent) Increase in the price of the product.

If the original product increases in price by this extent (5–10%) and consumers switch to buying an alternative product as a result, then both products will be found to share the same market and are readily interchangeable.

Case examples

Dominant

Microsoft

Microsoft had legal protection for the technical aspects of its operating system and included a music processor as part of the operating system.

Because technical aspects of the operating system were secret, it was difficult for manufacturers of other music processors to sell their products to anyone using the Microsoft operating system and ensure compatibility .

Given that Microsoft holds such a large share of the software market, the effect was to freeze competitors (for music processors) out of the market.

The Commission investigated the situation and found that Microsoft had abused its dominant position under Article 10.

It ordered Microsoft to release information on the relevant technical aspects of the operating system so that manufacturers of music processors could develop compatible products. The Commission also imposed a record fine of €497 million and imposed other penalties.

Not dominant

Continental Can

The company manufactured cans for meat and fish and metal lids for jars. The Commission investigated and decided that Continental Can was dominant in the market.

The Court ruled that the Commission had failed to take into account supply substitution and hence the time factor (RTM) in assessing dominance, and overruled the Commission finding.

The potential for supply substitution was high, it being easy for rival manufacturers of fruit or condensed milk cans to adapt their products and break into the Continental Can market.

Thus, it can be seen in the above cases that whereas *Microsoft* was in a clearly dominant position as the user has little choice over the supplier of operating systems and other Microsoft products, it was not the case in *Continental Can* where other manufacturers could quickly break into the market.

Spare parts

One way in which undertakings may be dominant is by producing spare parts for their main products such as ink cartridges for printers.

In trying to determine the RPM, it is necessary to consider whether the complementary products form part of the main (or primary) market or are part of a separate market. If there is a separate market, then an undertaking which is not dominant in the primary market may be dominant in the separate market.

The Commission or an NCA may therefore look at the spare parts market to establish whether dominance exists in that market specifically. What might, at first sight, appear to be an inconsequential market, can in fact amount to a sub-market in its own right.

| Hilti | → | The company tried to insist that retailers selling its nail guns had to sell its nail cartridges and nails (i.e. consumables) too. | → | In the consumables market, Hilti had a 70–80% share and were dominant. The CJ held that the market for the consumables was a separate market from the market for the product with which they were used. Hilti's attempt to tie in consumables with its major product in this way is also referred to as 'bundling'. |

Bundling is a key issue for the Commission as it indicates that potentially there is both a primary product market as well as a secondary product market, which the manufacturers can seek to dominate. Think of when you buy a printer and the usually high cost of the specialist replacement cartridges which only work with certain makes.

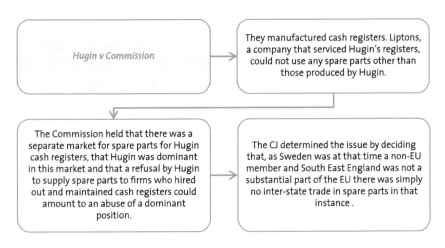

| *Hugin v Commission* | → | They manufactured cash registers. Liptons, a company that serviced Hugin's registers, could not use any spare parts other than those produced by Hugin. |
| The Commission held that there was a separate market for spare parts for Hugin cash registers, that Hugin was dominant in this market and that a refusal by Hugin to supply spare parts to firms who hired out and maintained cash registers could amount to an abuse of a dominant position. | → | The CJ determined the issue by deciding that, as Sweden was at that time a non-EU member and South East England was not a substantial part of the EU there was simply no inter-state trade in spare parts in that instance. |

Other factors to determine the RPM
Intended use of the product

**Case precedent – *Nederlandsche Banden-Industrie Michelin NV v Commission*
332/81 [1983] ECR 3461**

Facts: Michelin used a system of financial rebates and bonuses, the granting of which was not based on objective economic criteria. The Commission investigated the tyre market and found that there were a number of different markets for tyres, such as the 'replacement tyres for heavy vehicles', 'replacement tyres for light vehicles', 'tyres sold with new cars' and 'retread tyres'. If the market were structured in this way, Michelin would be held to be dominant in the market for tyres for heavy vehicles Michelin argued that the market should not be structured in that way; the whole market for tyres should be taken into account. If it were, Michelin would not be dominant.

Principle: The CJ looked at the intended use for the product, namely, tyres for heavy vehicles, and found that there was no interchangeability between different types of tyres (i.e. light vehicles and heavy vehicles use different types of tyres). Accordingly, it held that the RPM was the market for replacement tyres for heavy vehicles.

Application: This illustrates that markets can be sub-divided into smaller markets where dominance can be found.

Product as determined by marketing strategies

Case precedent – *BBI/Boosey & Hawkes*

Facts: The Commission identified a separate market called the British brass band instrument market, as distinct from the brass instrument market generally.

Principle: This was justified on the basis that the consumers were different in each market, the uses were different and, indeed, the marketing strategy of Boosey & Hawkes recognised that there were separate markets.

Application: By examining the intended user of the product and the associated marketing campaign, it is possible to get a better fix on the market (e.g. consider the marketing of a product you use: does this suggest the intended market)?

Relevant geographic market (RGM)

It is now time to turn the spotlight on the second market, the RGM, namely, where is the product sold?

Article 102 states that the dominant position of an undertaking accused of abuse must be '... within the common market or in a substantial part of it ...'. As a result of these words, it is necessary for the Commission to determine what the RGM is before dominance can be assessed.

As the EU exists to create one internal market, the RGM can generally be taken to be the whole of the internal market. However, there may be factors which cause the RGM to be determined more narrowly.

In *United Brands*, the CJ defined the RGM as 'an area where the objective conditions of competition applying to the product in question [are] the same for all traders'. Here the RGM was found to cover six Member States because in those states the product (and conditions of competition) were effectively the same for all traders. Three Member States, namely France, Italy and the UK, were excluded because they had special arrangements in relation to the banana trade with overseas territories.

As substantial market is assessed not just on geographical area but includes other factors such as volume of trade, the cases have demonstrated a wide range of RGMs.

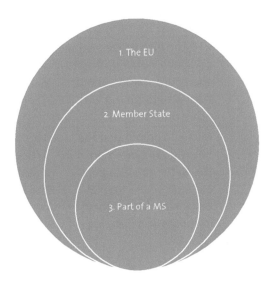

The EU: Definition of relevant geographic market

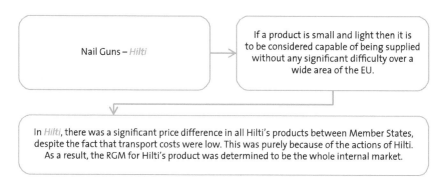

In *Hilti*, there was a significant price difference in all Hilti's products between Member States, despite the fact that transport costs were low. This was purely because of the actions of Hilti. As a result, the RGM for Hilti's product was determined to be the whole internal market.

The RGM will be determined by many factors including ease of transport, cultural usage, length of presence in the market etc, and can be the whole of the EU as in *Hilti* or smaller as below.

One Member State – Definition of RGM

It is also the case that undertakings, which only operate in one major territory, are likely to dominate in that area as below:

Case	Facts	Decision
British Telecommunications R V HM Treasury exp BT	BT had total control of the telephone industry in the UK and were refusing to allow competitors to use their telephone lines and cables.	This was a breach of Article 102. BT had a dominant position in the UK.
RTE RTE & ITP v Commission	RTE, the Irish broadcasting company were refusing to share information about their programming with other publishers.	This was a breach of Article 102. RTE had a dominant position in the Republic of Ireland.
Michelin Nederlandsche Banden-Industrie Michelin NV v Commission	Michelin dominated the heavy good tyres market in the Netherlands: a good example of the market being sub-divided for the purposes of Article 102.	This was a breach of Article 102. Michelin had a dominant position in the Netherlands.

Part of a Member State – Definition of RGM

The case law has also produced cases where the CJEU has decided that it is possible for only a part of a Member State to be a substantial part of the market.

Substantial part	Not a substantial part
The port of Holyhead, Wales • In *B&I Line plc v Sealink Harbours Ltd and Sealink Stena Ltd*, the port of Holyhead in North Wales was held to be a substantial part of the market because of the volume of trade between Eire and the UK	**South-east England** • In *Hugin*, South-east England was found not to be a 'substantial part' of the internal market, as there was not enough volume of trade to justify such a finding.

North-west Germany

• In *Continental Cans*, this was a substantial part of the market due to the potential volume of trade.

Relevant temporal market

In addition to the RPM and the RGM, it may also be necessary to establish how long an undertaking has been dominant or is likely to be dominant.

This is known as the 'relevant temporal market' or 'RTM'. In *Continental Cans*, the company proved that the Commission had not taken into account the fact that rival manufacturers of similar containers were likely to move into the market and that in such a fiercely competitive market, the company's dominance was transient.

Is there dominance?

Moving onto the second step in our diagram on p. 190, once the relevant market (RPM and RGM, and, where necessary, the RTM) has been established, the Commission or NCA must then determine if an undertaking is dominant in that market.

In *United Brands*, the CJ defined the meaning of dominance as follows:

> '. . . a position of economic strength enjoyed by an undertaking which enables it to prevent effective competition being maintained on the relevant market by giving it the power to behave to an appreciable extent independently of its competitors, customers, and ultimately, of its customers.

In order to assess dominance, the CJ has examined the following factors:

Relative share of the market	❖ *Tetrapak Rausing SA v Commission:* 90% of the relevant market ❖ *Continental Can:* 7–80% of the relevant market ❖ *Intel Corporation:* At least 70% of the x86 CPU chip market ❖ *Akzo Chemie BV v Commission:* over 50% of the relevant market ❖ *United Brands:* only 40–45% of the relevant RPM, yet was found to be dominant. The other factors that the Commission took into account in that case included that the relevant market was fragmented and the nearest rival held only a 17% market share.
Legal factors	❖ *Hugin* was the only company in the UK that manufactured spare parts for Hugin cash registers because the design for the cash registers was patented. ❖ *Tetrapak* had an exclusive patent licence over the design of the relevant cartons. In both these cases, the respective intellectual property rights made it difficult for other undertakings to enter into the markets and this reduced competition. ❖ *Microsoft* one of the penalties imposed upon the company was to break its IP protection over certain key codes which had to be supplied to rival software manufacturers.
Superior technology	❖ In both *Hoffmann-La Roche & Co v Commission* (vitamins) and *Michelin* (replacement tyres for heavy vehicles), the superior technology of the respective undertakings made it difficult for other undertakings to compete.
Wealth of capital	❖ *Akzo* produced a chemical that could be used in both the manufacture of flour and in the plastics industry. Sales to the plastics industry were much more profitable that those to the flour industry. In response to a rival undertaking, which had previously made the chemical exclusively for use in the flour industry, starting to sell its product to the plastics industry, Akzo reduced the price it charged for the chemical to the flour industry to below the average variable cost (i.e. the extent to which prices vary according to the amount manufactured). Akzo made a loss on each of these sales. Its intention was to drive the rival out of the market. The Commission held that this amounted to predatory pricing.

| Vertical integration | ❖ *United Brands* had control of the entire industry from growing the bananas to distribution and retail. This makes it easier for them to dominate. |

| Sophisticated distribution systems | ❖ *Hoffmann-La Roche* had a highly sophisticated sales network. Seemingly innocuous clauses in the company's contracts with distributors were found to present practical barriers to entry into the market by rival undertakings. For example, the so-called English clause allowed Hoffmann-La Roche's distributors to buy from rival suppliers even if the rivals offered prices lower than Hoffmann-La Roche, provided that the distributors gave Hoffmann-La Roche the marketing information from the rival undertaking and allowed Hoffmann-La Roche the opportunity to match the lower prices. Although such a clause may seem fair (indeed, the distributors had not complained about it), the Commission argued successfully that the effect of the clause was to close the market to rivals. Because Hoffmann-La Roche were in such a dominant position, the company could always match the lower prices and could continue to do so until the rival's attempt to break into the market failed. |

| Brand identification | ❖ *United Brands:* The Commission established that consumers associated the United Brands' Chiquita trademark with bananas, as a result of heavy marketing by United Brands. |

Does the conduct amount to abuse?

The dominance of a market, in itself, does not amount to a breach of Article 102. There must be an abuse of a dominant position. Many types of business practice can amount to abusive behaviour. Generally, if behaviour differs from that governing normal competition on the basis of performance, it can engage by Article 102.

However, for a dominant undertaking even seemingly normal competitive behaviour may be caught unless it can be objectively justified. A dominant undertaking must not behave so as to damage the competitive market in general, because the Commission considers that such undertakings have a 'special responsibility' not to distort genuine competition.

Article 102 sets out a list of some specific types of behaviour that may amount to abuse. These include unfair pricing, limiting production, contractual discrimination and imposing supplementary obligations. This list is non-exhaustive.

Case precedent – The Commission's Decision on *Intel Corporation* (ref IP/09/745) in May 2009

Facts: Intel Corp was fined the current record fine of €1.06 billion for providing a system of generous rebates to Acer, Dell, HP, Lenovo and NEC in return for buying all or nearly all of their x86 CPU chips from Intel rather than the rival AMD (Advanced Micro Devices) Corporation.

They also made direct payments to a chain of stores (Media Markt) on condition that it only stocked computers containing Intel chips. As a result it was so difficult for AMD to enter this particular market that even its most competitive offers would not be taken up.

When it offered to supply one million of its chips free to a computer manufacturer the manufacturer turned it down as losing the Intel rebate would have involved a greater loss of money than it stood to gain by accepting the free chips.

Principle: The Commission argued that as a result the ability of rivals to compete and innovate was impaired leading to a reduction of choice on the market to the disadvantage of consumers. Given Intel's 70% dominance, the Commission had little difficulty concluding that rebates that are conditional on buying less of a rivals products, or none at all, must be abusive unless Intel could produce justifiable reasons.

Application: In its decision the Commission did not object to rebates in themselves (which can often advantage the consumer) but to the conditions attached to those rebates illustrating that it may be the effects of the behaviour in the context of dominance which constitutes an abuse under Article 102.

Any behaviour by a dominant undertaking that is designed to exclude or drive a competitor from the market will be held to be abusive, as will any behaviour that seeks to exploit or take unfair advantage in some way of the dominant position.

Types of abuse

Abuse	Name	Rationale
Refusal to supply	*Commercial Solvents Corportation (CSC) v Commission*	The refusal by Commercial Solvents to supply a competitor with the material necessary for the manufacture of an end product was held to be abusive.
	United Brands	Certain clauses (called the 'Green Banana' clauses) in its contracts with distributors were found to amount to abuse. These clauses sought to control the length of time that bananas remained under the control of United Brands. The clauses operated to ensure that bananas were not sold on to other companies until they had only a very short remaining shelf life.
	B&I/Sealink	Sealink used its control of the port of Holyhead to give better sailing times to its own ferries.
Supplementary obligations	*Microsoft*	The decision has established the criteria needed for bundling to amount to an offence under Article 102(d) TFEU as follows: the tying and tied goods must not be within the same product market; the undertaking must be dominant in the tying product market; customers get no choice whether to accept the tied product with the tying product; and the tying closes out any competition.
Imposing unfair prices	*Tetrapak*	The dominant undertaking uses its financial strength to fund the price cuts and drive rivals out of the market. While difficult to define in economic terms, the CJ typically has found predatory pricing to exist where either the price has been pushed below cost price or where the intention in reducing the price has simply been to remove competition.
	United Brands	Different customers are charged different prices for the same product. Some price differences are acceptable if they can be justified by objective market forces such as different labour costs in different parts of the EU.

Abuse	Name	Rationale
Rebates	*Intel*	These may amount to abusive behaviour where they are not linked to objective market forces. Such rebates can stop a competitor entering the market because the competitor cannot match the rebated (or reduced) prices.
	Hoffmann-La Roche	Provided fidelity rebates on its prices in return for consumers buying the relevant products only from it. In its judgment, the CJ stated: 'The fidelity rebate, unlike quantity rebates exclusively linked with the volume of purchases from the producer concerned, is designed through the grant of a financial advantage to prevent customers from obtaining their supplies from competing producers.'

Does this abuse affect trade between Member States?

The final element of an offence under Article 102 (as with Article 101) is that the abuse of the dominant position must 'affect trade between Member States'. It is sufficient that such behaviour might affect such trade.

Case precedent – *British Leyland v Commission*

Facts: Excessive and discriminatory fees were charged for type-approval certificates for left-hand drive motor vehicles, without any objective economic justification.

Principle: The CJ held that it was not necessary to establish any specific effect on trade. Evidence that abuse might affect trade was enough.

Application: This illustrates the ability of the EU to find a potential breach of the Article, not just a finding on an actual abuse of dominance indicating how central this law is to the EU.

'The problem with the . . . [punishment] . . . of market power *per se* is that it may well be undesirable because the dominant firm may have attained this position through superior efficiency and lower costs. We would therefore be penalising the winner of the competitive race even though the victory was achieved through legitimate means.' (*Craig and de Burca EU Law: Texts, Cases and Materials 5th edn.*)

Putting it into practice

Competition Law 2: Art 102

Critically evaluate how the Community institutions have developed the relevant areas of EU Law, specifically Article 102 TFEU, to balance and control market power without resorting to outright punishment for simply possessing it.

Suggested solution

This essay question asks you to focus on the approach to the abuse of a dominant position in the EU with a specific focus on Article 102 TFEU. One issue here to avoid is the simple listing and explaining of the law without making critical comments throughout.

Introduction
In such a question, it is useful to refer to the quotation in your introduction and broadly but concisely set out the key theme; in this case that there is a potential tension between free competition and the EU laws on competition

Art 102 Key elements	
1 Dominant market position 2 Abuse of this 3 Affecting the market	You should explain these in outline making the critical point that dominance by itself is not enough – all three elements must be found – relate this to the essay question.

Dominant market position	
Explain in detail the RPM, RGM and RTM with case law support; *United Brands* etc	Critically analyse, perhaps pointing out the differences in opinion between the alleged offending companies and the authorites.

Abuse	
Illustrate through case law what has been found to be abusive behaviour by firms: *Hilti, Akzo* etc.	This provides a good opportunity to critically discuss the nature of this Article and the approach of the competition authorities to this area.

Affecting the market	
Give examples of how abuse of a dominant position affects the market: *Microsoft*	You can make the point here that this area is regarded so seriously that potentialy affecting the market is also included: *BT*.

Conclusion
Throughout the essay you should have been able to both outline the law and make some critical comments. This will allow you to conclude: does the EU have the balance right by affording valuable protection or is competition law a hindrance to innovation and entrepreneurs?

Table of key cases referred to in this chapter

Case name	Area of law	Principle
Akzo Chemie BV v Commission C62/86 [1991] ECR I-3359	Dominance and abuse	A market share over 50%.
BBI/Boosey & Hawkes Decision 87/500 [1987] OJ L286/36; [1988] 4 CMLR 67	Intended market share	The marketing strategy indicated the intended market.
B&I Line plc v Sealink Harbours Ltd and Sealink Stena Ltd [1992] 5 CMLR 255	RGM	A port with substantial trade could form the RGM.
British Leyland v Commission C226/84 [1986] ECR 3263	Effect on trade	Potential abuse is also covered.
Commerical SolventsCorporation (CSC) v Commission C6 & 7/73 [1974] ECR 223	Abuse	Refusal to supply amounted to abuse.

Euroemballage Corn and Continental Can Co Ltd C6/72 [1973] ECR 215	RTM	The company may not be dominant for very long due to the nature of their product.
Hilti AG v Commission T30/89A [1990] ECR II-163 and C53/92P [1994] ECR I-667	RPM	The Commission decided on a narrow RPM.
Hoffmann-La Roche & Co v Commission C85/76 [1979] ECR 461	Dominance and abuse	Superior technology coupled with fidelity rebates equalled a breach of Article 102.
Hugin v Commission C22/78 [1979] ECR 1869	Spare parts	The company had a part in both primary and secondary markets.
Intel Corporation (Decision IP/09/745)	Dominance and abuse	Loyalty discounts amounted to abuse along with 70% market share.
Microsoft Case COMP/C- 3/37.792	RPM	Dominating the software market and accused of 'bundling'.
Nederlandsche Banden-Industrie Michelin NV v Commission C332/81 [1983] ECR 3461	RPM	The RPM was a particular type of tyre not the general tyre market.
R v HM Treasury exp BT C392/93 [1996] ECR I-6131	RGM	BT dominated in the UK alone.
RTE & ITP v Commission T69 and 76/89 [1991] ECR II-485	RGM	RTE had a dominant market share in the Republic of Ireland.
Tetrapak Rausing SA v Commission T51/8 [1990] ECR II-309	Dominance and abuse	A huge market share plus huge undercutting of the prices of rivals.
United Brands v Commission C27/76 [1978] ECR 207	RPM	Dominant in the narrower banana market (not the wider fruit).

@ **Visit the book's companion website to test your knowledge**

❖ Resources include a subject map, revision tip podcasts, downloadable diagrams, MCQ quizzes for each chapter, and a flashcard glossary

❖ www.routledge.com/cw/optimizelawrevision

Index